The forensic use of bioinformation: ethical issues

NUFFIELD
COUNCIL ON
BIOETHICS

Nuffield Council on Bioethics

The terms of reference of the Council are:

1 to identify and define ethical questions raised by recent advances in biological and medical research in order to respond to, and to anticipate, public concern;

2 to make arrangements for examining and reporting on such questions with a view to promoting public understanding and discussion; this may lead, where needed, to the formulation of new guidelines by the appropriate regulatory or other body;

3 in the light of the outcome of its work, to publish reports; and to make representations, as the Council may judge appropriate.

The Nuffield Council on Bioethics is funded jointly by the Medical Research Council, the Nuffield Foundation and the Wellcome Trust

Foreword

This Report deals with some discrete issues at the cusp of current controversies about the proper balance between police powers and individual rights to liberty, autonomy and privacy. In what circumstances should the police be permitted to take fingerprints and DNA samples, and for how long should they be able to retain them and the resulting DNA profiles? How should DNA and fingerprint evidence be used in criminal trials? When is it ethically acceptable to use the National DNA Database (NDNAD) for familial searching, inferring ethnicity and non-operational research purposes? What systems of governance and regulation are necessary?

Our starting point is that, while the science and technology of DNA profiling and fingerprinting are, for the most part, increasingly robust and reliable, mistakes can and do occur. We make recommendations that are designed to reduce the risks of mistaken identification and wrongful conviction which may result from the (relatively rare) cases of flawed science and the (more frequent) failure of experts to present the scientific evidence in ways that can be properly understood by legal professionals and juries.

In dealing with the central questions of police powers to obtain biological evidence, to retain it, and to search DNA and fingerprint databases for various purposes, our main theme is proportionality: that the presumption in a liberal democracy in favour of individual liberty, autonomy, privacy, informed consent and equal treatment can be overcome only for other legitimate ends (such as public security), and where there is relevant and compelling empirical evidence that the means are proportionate. To ensure that this is the case, and that it is managed in a transparent fashion, effective governance and regulation are essential.

In making our recommendations, we are aware that fingerprinting and DNA profiling are part of a wider range of rapidly developing biometric technologies that have the potential for being combined into multi-modal identification systems. We are also aware that these technologies have other applications, such as in public health, medical and scientific research, immigration and passport systems, and for personal and corporate use. We have confined ourselves to an old (fingerprinting) and a new (DNA) technology in the context of criminal justice, both to keep the discussion within manageable proportions, and because this is currently the area of greatest controversy, but of little informed, in-depth study. Our aim is to provide a sound, principled analysis based on the available evidence.

We have been greatly assisted by responses to the public consultation (see Appendix 2), and by a series of fact-finding meetings and a workshop with key stakeholders (see Appendix 1). We benefited from discussions with colleagues on the French National Consultative Bioethics Committee for Health and Life Sciences and the German National Ethics Council. (The French Committee published an Opinion (No. 98) entitled *Biometrics, identifying data and human rights* in April 2007, see Appendix 5.)

I would like to express my personal thanks, and those of the Council, to the members of the Working Group, who gave unstintingly of their time and energy, and who worked patiently through many drafts, in order to produce this Report. Five peer reviewers made substantial comments, which we have tried to take into account. Our Project Manager, Carole McCartney of the University of Leeds, brought to her task not only her own expertise in this field but also an infectious enthusiasm, dedication and sense of humour, which enabled us to complete a substantial report within nine months. Thanks are also due to other members of the Secretariat, in particular Hugh Whittall, Catherine Moody, Harald Schmidt, Katharine Wright and Caroline Rogers, who have worked hard to bring this to fruition.

Professor Sir Bob Hepple QC FBA

Bob Hepple

Acknowledgements

The Council would like to thank the members of the Working Group for their considerable expertise and commitment in producing this Report. The Council is also grateful to a number of people who reviewed an earlier version: Professor Sarah Cunningham-Burley, Professor Mark Jobling, Professor Mike Parker, Professor Paul Roberts and Professor Mark Rothstein. We thank those who attended or hosted fact-finding meetings, including: Karen Squibb-Williams, Robert Green, Mike McMullen, Dr Ric Treble, David Charlton, Simon Moore, Geoff Whitaker, Matthew Greenhalgh, David Hartshorne, Tracy Shannon and Dr Colin Kimpton. The Working Group and the Council convey appreciation and thanks to all those who responded to the consultation by providing insightful and valuable submissions (see Appendix 2). We thank staff at the National Policing Improvement Agency (NPIA), in particular Andrew Davies, for providing helpful and timely answers to all questions put to him.

Members of the Working Group

Professor Sir Bob Hepple QC FBA (Chair)

Emeritus Master of Clare College and Emeritus Professor of Law, University of Cambridge; Chairman of the Nuffield Council on Bioethics

Mr Graham Cooke

Barrister, King's Bench Chambers, Bournemouth

Professor Søren Holm

Professorial Fellow in Bioethics, University of Cardiff; Member of the Council

Professor Graeme Laurie

Professor of Law, University of Edinburgh

Dr Bronwyn Parry

Reader in Social and Cultural Geography, Queen Mary, University of London; Member of the Council

Professor Andrew Read

Chair of Human Genetics, University of Manchester

Professor Robin Williams

Professor of Sociology, University of Durham

Terms of reference

1 To identify and consider the ethical, social and legal issues raised by current and potential future uses of bioinformation for forensic purposes.

2 To consider, in particular:

a) the interpretation of the information;

b) the collection, storage and retention of profiles and samples;

c) issues of informed consent, privacy and confidentiality in the light of data protection and human rights legislation;

d) arguments for and against population-wide forensic databases;

e) access to and use of forensic databases for purposes of research;

f) admissibility and use of bioinformation in criminal proceedings;

g) sharing of bioinformation for forensic purposes across international boundaries;

h) use for forensic purposes of bioinformation collected for non-forensic purposes; and

i) governance of research conducted by or for forensic laboratories.

3 To identify the ethical and legal principles and procedures which should govern the forensic use of bioinformation, and to make recommendations.

4 To draft a Report on these issues.

Table of contents

Chapter 4 – Criminal investigation

Chapter 5 – Trial

Chapter 6 – Familial searching, inferring ethnicity and research uses

Chapter 7 – Governance and ethical oversight

Executive summary

Introduction (Chapter 1)

1 The development over the past two decades of the science of deoxyribonucleic acid (DNA) profiling has led to a dramatic increase in the forensic use of bioinformation. Together with the older use of fingerprints and other emergent biometric technologies, there is growing potential for combining data to produce multi-modal identification systems. Police powers to take and retain fingerprints and biological samples have been steadily widened by a series of Acts of Parliament. Today the police of England and Wales have wider sampling powers than those in any other country, and the United Kingdom has proportionally, per head of population, the largest forensic DNA database in the world, with approximately four million samples (or about six per cent of the population), while the national fingerprint database holds over 6.5 million fingerprint records from individuals.

The interpretation of bioinformation (Chapter 2)

2 Recent cases have highlighted concerns about fingerprinting techniques, and there is controversy over the standard required before a true 'match' between a fingerprint found at a crime scene and one taken from a suspect can be declared. However, once a match is made, fingerprint evidence generally remains unassailable in the criminal courts as a unique identifier (see paragraph 2.2).

3 In general, the science and technology of DNA profiling is increasingly robust and reliable. However, there remain risks, especially when the scientific techniques are pushed to their limits. In particular there are dangers of deliberate or accidental contamination, misinterpretation of mixed samples (those originating from more than one person), mistaken interpretation of partial profiles and the misuse of statistics to establish the probability of a match. Our recommendations in the following chapters are designed to reduce the risks of mistaken identification resulting from (relatively rare) cases of flawed science. We also recommend that the regulatory authorities should require and rigorously monitor quality assurance, and support independent research into new scientific techniques and technologies that are likely to improve reliability and accuracy.

Ethical values and human rights (Chapter 3)

4 The protection of the public from criminal activities is a primary obligation of the state. In a liberal democracy, such as the United Kingdom, it is also necessary to protect several fundamental ethical values and to respect modern legislation on human rights. The values with which we are primarily concerned are *liberty, autonomy, privacy, informed consent* and *equality*. These values are not absolute but there is a strong presumption in liberal democracies in favour of not restricting them. We broadly endorse a rights-based approach that both recognises the fundamental importance to human beings of respect for their individual liberty, autonomy and privacy, and the need, in appropriate circumstances, to restrict these rights either in the general interest or to protect the rights of others.

5 It is clear that well-functioning forensic databases have the potential to promote the public interest to a significant degree, but to argue convincingly that this justifies overriding identifiable personal interests or rights requires a number of further steps. The principle of *proportionality*, which is relevant in both ethical and legal debates, is thus at the heart of many of the recommendations in this Report. The legally enforceable human rights that are relevant to our justifications include the right to a *fair trial*, the right to *respect for private*

and family life, and the right to *equal treatment*. Any interference with these rights must be *proportionate*.

Criminal investigation (Chapter 4)

Taking fingerprints and biological samples

6 Fingerprints and DNA samples may be taken from suspects, victims or witnesses in the course of criminal investigations. If an individual has been arrested in connection with a 'recordable' offence[1], the present law in the United Kingdom permits the police discretion to take fingerprints and biological samples without the consent of the individual. Many of those arrested for these offences may have committed other offences. Thus the taking of samples from them raises the possibility of identifying suspects for unsolved prior offences from which biological material was obtained. **It is our view that the authority to take (for impending use in criminal investigation) fingerprints and biological samples without consent from those who are arrested on suspicion of involvement in any recordable offence is proportionate to the aim of detecting and prosecuting crime. At the same time, we note that the distinction between recordable and non-recordable offences is to some extent arbitrary (e.g. failing to give advance notice of a procession is recordable, but obstruction of the highway is not). We recommend that the list of recordable offences for which fingerprints and biological samples can be taken from arrestees, should be rationalised so as to exclude all minor, non-imprisonable offences** (paragraph 4.17).

7 Home Office proposals announced in March 2007 suggested that the police may in future be permitted to take and store fingerprints and biological samples from any arrestee, regardless of whether or not the offence was recordable. This would extend sampling to people who may have been arrested on suspicion of minor offences, such as minor traffic offences, littering or begging. With this potential further extension of police powers, the National DNA Database (NDNAD) could expand dramatically, rapidly encompassing a fifth or more of the population. **It is our view that the authority of the police to take and store both fingerprints and biological samples from all arrestees without their consent, regardless of the reason for the arrest, is disproportionate to the aims of identifying a person and of confirming whether or not a person was at a crime scene. Suspicion of involvement in a minor (at present 'non-recordable') offence does not justify the taking of bioinformation from individuals without their consent** (paragraph 4.23).

8 Police powers to take bioinformation are no longer confined to use within a police station. Indeed, the recent introduction of hand-held devices that can check fingerprints against the national fingerprint database, has led to the ability of the police to check the identification of individuals already on the database 'on-the-spot'. **Where fingerprints are taken electronically in order to verify an identity, they should be compared only with stored subject records and destroyed once such a check has been completed** (paragraph 4.23).

Retaining biological samples, DNA profiles and fingerprints

9 The retention of fingerprints, DNA profiles and biological samples is generally more controversial than the taking of such bioinformation, and the retention of biological samples raises greater ethical concerns than digitised DNA profiles and fingerprints (given the differences in the level of information that could be revealed). The Criminal Justice Act 2003 extended indefinite retention both of fingerprints and biological samples to all those

1. All offences which carry the possibility of a custodial sentence are recordable (or 'notifiable'), plus 52 other, non-imprisonable offences specified in the Schedule to the National Police Records (Recordable Offences) (Amendment) Regulations 2005 (SI 2005/3106). See Box 1.2.

arrested for recordable offences in England and Wales, even if they are subsequently acquitted. The Home Office proposals (published in March 2007) mentioned above would allow such retention from *all* arrestees. The criminal justice systems of many European countries do not have such wide powers of retention as England and Wales. For example, in Scotland indefinite retention of both the profile and the subject sample is allowed only on conviction of an offence, with the exception of time-limited retention in the case of charge for sexual or violent offences. In all other cases, samples and information derived from them must be destroyed if the arrestee is not convicted of an offence or otherwise subject to judicial disposal.

10 The retention of fingerprints or DNA profiles does not (at this time) permit the police to derive directly more detailed information about an individual. In particular, a fingerprint cannot reveal information about an individual, and the DNA profiles currently produced are limited, making it difficult for the profile to reveal further, or sensitive, information (see Chapter 2 for details). It is, however, entirely possible to sequence all or part of an individual's genome from their biological sample, and therefore, the retention of biological samples requires much greater critical attention, and justification. It is our view that electronic retention of fingerprints and DNA profiles is much less contentious than the retention of biological samples and incurs very little cost. However, there is, at present, a lack of convincing evidence that retention of profiles of those not charged with or convicted of an offence has had a significant impact on detection rates and hence it is difficult to argue that such retention can be justified. **Accordingly we recommend that independent research should be commissioned by the Home Office to assess the impact of retention. In the light of the findings of that research, an informed judgment could then be made** (paragraph 4.53).

11 Our approach to the retention of fingerprints, profiles and biological samples is guided by the principle of proportionality, bearing in mind the purpose of retaining bioinformation on the one hand, and, on the other, the absence of satisfactory empirical evidence to justify the present practice of retaining indefinitely such information from all those who are arrested for a recordable offence, irrespective of whether they are subsequently charged or convicted. We note that in Scotland and most other European countries such retention is not considered necessary. We also recognise that there are personal implications for individuals whose profiles are on the NDNAD as a result of being implicated in a crime, but who were subsequently found to be innocent (see paragraphs 3.24–3.26). Moreover, in the case of retention of samples, this is not only expensive, but it is also the focus of considerable public concern about possible future uses to which the samples might be put. **We recommend that the law in England, Wales and Northern Ireland should be brought into line with that in Scotland. Fingerprints, DNA profiles and subject biological samples should be retained indefinitely only for those convicted of a recordable offence. At present, the retention of profiles and samples can be justified as proportionate only for those who have been convicted. In all other cases, samples should be destroyed and the resulting profiles deleted from the NDNAD. This should be reviewed in the light of the findings of the further research that we have recommended** (paragraph 4.54).

12 **The Scottish practice of allowing retention of samples and profiles, for three years, from those charged with serious violent or sexual offences, even if there is no conviction, should also be followed. Thereafter the samples and profiles should be destroyed unless a Chief Constable applies to a court for a two-year extension, showing reasonable grounds for the extension** (paragraph 4.55).

13 The costs of sampling increasing numbers of individuals, maintaining an expanding database, and storing millions of biological samples will continue to escalate, yet there is little supportive empirical evidence that demonstrates significant benefits in terms of crime

detection. An alternative policy may be to dedicate more resources to developing clear auditing processes to demonstrate the worth of the NDNAD and IDENT1 (the software platform that hosts the national fingerprint database), while ensuring that there are processes in place to exploit fully the bioinformation already available to the police, and to prioritise the collection of bioinformation from crime scenes, rather than individuals. At present, fewer than 20 per cent of crime scenes are forensically examined, and only a small proportion of these yield any biological material that is then tested. **In light of the discussion of the usefulness of bioinformation in the investigation of crime, we recommend that:**

- **Expenditure for expert crime scene analysis should be given higher priority than the increased collection of subject samples. If the Government is right to assert that "the whole of the active suspect criminal population is now held on the NDNAD", then further improvements in DNA detection rates rest heavily on expanding crime scene collection rates and ensuring that full use is made of the material collected.**
- **There should be improved recording of police data on the uses of DNA matches and the production of better statistics to inform key stakeholders and the wider public. More effort should also be made to ascertain 'best practice' within policing to maximise the crime control potential of bioinformation. The collation of statistics would also assist with an exploration of the cost-effectiveness of the forensic use of bioinformation and may provide evidence as to whether infringements on the liberty, privacy and autonomy of individuals are justified.**
- **To justify the interference with the liberty and autonomy of citizens, more detailed independent research on the contribution of bioinformation to criminal justice is required** (paragraph 4.35).

14 Samples obtained from crime scenes are not currently retained once a conviction has been secured in relation to an offence and a decision has been made that it will no longer be investigated. Permanent retention of crime scene samples would permit not only the possible identification of further potential suspects who may have been involved in an offence, but also allow for the possibility of rectifying possible miscarriages of justice in the future. **We therefore recommend that, because crime scene samples are unique and unrepeatable, they must be retained indefinitely** (paragraph 4.56).

Volunteers

15 Volunteers (who may be victims, witnesses or volunteers in mass intelligence screens) may consent at the time of sampling to their profiles being permanently loaded onto the NDNAD. This decision is currently irrevocable. Such an approach is contrary to standard practice in medical research, and differs from practice in Scotland and many other European countries, where consent can be withdrawn. It has been reported to us that up to 40 per cent of people who voluntarily provide elimination samples also consent (irrevocably) to having their sample stored permanently and their profile loaded onto the NDNAD where it will be used in speculative searches for the indefinite future. If true, we believe that such a level of consent may be lower if it were fully informed and properly considered.

16 **It is our view that consent given by a volunteer to retain their biological samples and resulting profile on the NDNAD must be revocable at any time and without any requirement to give a reason. This is a basic principle in all medical research and should equally apply to the voluntary component of the NDNAD, as it already does to the Scottish DNA Database. In view of the importance of this principle, we recommend that as a matter of policy, volunteers should not be asked to consent to the permanent storage of elimination biological samples and retention of DNA profiles derived from these samples beyond the conclusion of the relevant case** (paragraph 4.62).

Ethnic minorities

17 Policing priorities and practices may lead to the disproportionate arrest of certain populations. Attention has focused in particular on the over-representation of members of black minority ethnic groups and the number of young persons (under 18) without criminal records on bioinformation databases.

18 **In our view, the disproportionate over-representation of black ethnic minorities on the NDNAD is a matter of considerable concern, even if this arises from policing practice in making arrests rather than a fault with the NDNAD. Such disparities increase the risk of stigmatisation attendant on being known to have a profile on the NDNAD and can potentially lead to further alienation of whole minority ethnic communities. We therefore welcome the commissioning of an equality impact assessment by the NDNAD. This impact assessment should reveal the extent to which it is the discretionary use of powers of arrest or the use of sampling powers that contributes to over-representation of black ethnic minorities. The NDNAD and police forces may then be put under a positive obligation to take effective steps to address this over-representation. The promotion of equality of opportunity entails active steps to remove any practices that unjustifiably cause disparities between different groups** (paragraph 4.66).

Minors

19 While it is unsurprising that young people are over-represented on forensic databases in light of the peak age of offending, this has provoked criticism. In our view, the policy of permanently retaining the bioinformation of minors is particularly sensitive in the United Kingdom, where the age of criminal responsibility is low (at age ten years in England and Wales and eight in Scotland) compared with many other countries. It may be argued that retaining bioinformation from young people is contrary to Article 40 of the UN Convention on the Rights of the Child, in that the Convention requires special attention to be given to the treatment of children by legal systems, to protect them from stigma, and that if they have offended, opportunities for rehabilitation should be maximised. The destruction of relevant criminal justice records and accompanying body samples could become one element in such a rehabilitative process.

20 **When considering requests for the removal of profiles from the NDNAD and the destruction of biological samples taken from minors (including from adults who were minors when their DNA was taken), we recommend that there should be a presumption in favour of the removal of all records, fingerprints and DNA profiles, and the destruction of samples. In deciding whether or not the presumption has been rebutted, account should be taken of factors such as:**

- **the seriousness of the offence;**
- **previous arrests;**
- **the outcome of the arrest;**
- **the likelihood of this individual re-offending;**
- **the danger to the public; and**
- **any other special circumstances** (paragraph 4.72).

A population-wide database

21 There is recurrent public discussion of the potential for a population-wide DNA database, which would maximise forensic profiling abilities for the police while addressing concerns about discrimination. However, the increased intrusion into privacy that this would entail

would be compensated by only a negligible increase in public safety. In addition, there are also broader concerns that such a development would significantly shift the relationship between the individual and the state in that it might identify all individuals as potential offenders rather than as citizens of good will and benign intent.

22 **Currently, the balance of argument and evidence presented to us is against the establishment of a population-wide forensic DNA database. We conclude that such a response would be:**

- **disproportionate to the need to control crime;**
- **unlikely to secure public support; and**
- **impractical for the collection of samples from different categories of persons (such as visitors to the United Kingdom).**

However, the possibility of its establishment should be subject to review as biometric technology develops, and in the light of research on the potential contribution of such a database, under appropriate safeguards, to public safety and the detection of crime, and its potential for reducing discriminatory practices (paragraph 4.79).

Trial (Chapter 5)

23 Scientific techniques assist in the administration of justice only where the bioinformation used in a prosecution is robust, and is interpreted and represented accurately. Often it may have little or no evidential value: for example, in an assault where self-defence is raised. Further, serious doubts remain about the use of statistics in criminal proceedings. Scientific evidence, and the accompanying statistical data, may not (yet) be properly understood by non-experts involved in criminal proceedings, such as jurors, or even barristers, solicitors and judges.

24 During the pre-trial stages, in order that a defendant has the opportunity to challenge a fingerprint or DNA match, or its interpretation, it is vital that all DNA and fingerprint evidence is disclosed in a timely manner to both the defence and prosecution. Previous miscarriages of justice have highlighted the problem of non-disclosure of evidence to the defence. **We recommend:**

- **Compulsory and timely disclosure of *all* fingerprint bureau or DNA laboratory results and relevant records to all parties involved, including details of any dispute over an identification, rather than presenting only the consensus view reached.**
- **In expert witness statements and reports, this duty of disclosure should be explicitly acknowledged and the experts should confirm that they have complied with this duty** (paragraph 5.9).

25 It has become clear that fingerprint evidence can no longer be presented in court as if it were a simple statement of fact that there is a match between a crime scene mark and an accused person's print. Expert evidence which identifies marks linking an accused person to a scene of crime is evidence of opinion based on examination of the materials using the skill and experience of the expert. **We recommend that in presenting their opinion regarding a positive match or otherwise to the investigating officer, prosecution authority or court, fingerprint experts should make it clear that their conclusion is always one of expert judgment, and never a matter of absolute scientific certainty** (paragraph 5.15).

26 The 'prosecutor's fallacy' has compromised the use of DNA evidence for a fair trial. This fallacy suggests that the rarity of a profile is interchangeable with the probability that the defendant is innocent (for example the rarity of a one in a million match produces the false

conclusion that the chance of the defendant being innocent is one in a million).

27 Popular media representations of the power of fingerprint or DNA evidence may exacerbate difficulties in courtrooms. There are risks that, while a DNA match cannot be used without other evidence in a prosecution, it may be given undue weight in the courts. High expectations of the significance of bioinformation in forensics make essential the proper education of legal professionals throughout the criminal justice system, to prevent the misrepresentation of evidence, or at least to ensure the recognition of flawed or misrepresented evidence.

28 **In view of the difficulties with the presentation of complex statistical information in the courtroom, we recommend:**

- **that professionals (including judges) working within the criminal justice system should acquire a minimum standard of understanding of statistics, particularly with regard to DNA evidence;**
- **that trial judges ensure statistical evidence is accurately presented during trials, and that the decision in the *R v Doheny and (Gary) Adams* (1997) 1 Cr. App. R. 369 judgment regarding the correct presentation of DNA evidence is adhered to; and**
- **that in all cases where bioinformation evidence is adduced, introductory information should be made available to jury members, to ensure some basic understanding of the capabilities, and also the limitations, of such evidence** (paragraph 5.34).

Familial searching, inferring ethnicity, and research (Chapter 6)

29 The law makes clear that bioinformation stored on forensic databases may only be used for purposes related to preventing, detecting and prosecuting crime, or identifying a deceased person or a body part. This is, however, open to wide interpretation, and thus its original use for matching DNA profiles of suspects with crime scene samples has been extended by familial searching, inferring ethnicity and non-operational research.

Familial searching

30 When a crime scene profile does not match exactly any profile on the NDNAD, it is possible to look for 'partial' matches, which might mean that the crime scene stain was left by a (genetic) relative of a person whose profile partially matches the crime scene sample. This 'familial searching' technique can produce very many possible partial matches, severely limiting its usefulness. Because familial searching identifies a pool of possible genetic relatives of a suspect, it may thus produce sensitive information about biological relationships between individuals that may be unknown to the individuals concerned.

31 The aim of familial searching may be to legitimately provide useful intelligence in crime solving and there may be instances in which its use can be justified (see paragraph 6.11). However, before the technique is implemented on a wide scale, clear and explicit guidelines on its use must be introduced and made public, with adequate safeguards to protect against any possible unwarranted intrusion into family privacy. **While we do not believe that familial searching interferes with privacy rights to an extent that should prohibit its use (see paragraphs 3.3–3.7), it is our view that the potential benefits for crime detection must be balanced carefully with any potential for harm. The lack of consent obtained when sampling makes the use of the NDNAD in searching for relatives particularly sensitive. It is important therefore that this technique is not used unless it is necessary and proportionate in a particular case. Before it is more widely deployed, there needs to be detailed and independent research on its operational usefulness and on the practical consequences for those affected by it** (paragraph 6.11).

Inferring ethnicity

32 A statistical process can be applied to a DNA profile obtained from a crime scene stain, with the aim of predicting the 'ethnic appearance' of the unidentified individual to whom the DNA profile relates. The use of such a technique provides only an inference for use during a police investigation, for example reducing the size of a suspect 'pool', priority setting, or supporting or contradicting any witness statements. Although an ethnic inference is not used as prosecution evidence, significant ethical and practical concerns remain. Drawing an ethnic inference may lead police to narrow the focus of their enquiries prematurely, and there remains an anxiety that the current system of classification of people into seven 'ethnic appearances' may reinforce existing prejudice and racist generalisations about the likely perpetrators of crime. **In view of the significant ethical and practical problems, and the limited usefulness of the information provided, attempts to infer ethnicity from DNA profiles and samples fail the test of proportionality and we recommend that ethnic inferences should not be routinely sought, and should be used with great caution** (paragraph 6.17).

Non-operational research

33 Many of the uses of the NDNAD and stored samples can be classified as 'operational', in that the use is directly related to particular police investigations. However, the NDNAD and stored samples can also be used for other research purposes (in relation to forensics or crime) and in this context it is important to distinguish between the use of digital profiles and the use of the physical biological samples. Expanding use of the NDNAD makes crucial the need to introduce robust forms of ethical oversight and governance, particularly in instances where researchers use archived biological samples.

34 In deciding whether to permit research using the NDNAD and stored samples, the NDNAD Strategy Board considers whether there is a police need for the specified purpose, and the legality and ethical aspects of that purpose. Given the great sensitivity surrounding the use of genetics and the potential for harm, we recommend that any such proposals should be subjected to close ethical review. **We make a general recommendation that all research proposals using the NDNAD and stored samples should be formally, independently and transparently evaluated** (paragraph 6.21).

35 There are potentially a variety of research activities that could be performed using the resources of the NDNAD, including research into genetic markers of ethnicity, or genetically associated behavioural traits which may impact upon or influence criminality. **While recognising the potential value of research into genetic behavioural traits and ethnicity, in common with all other non-operational research, proposals in these areas must be subject to robust ethical scrutiny. The scientific credibility of the proposed research must be evaluated, examining, for example, the extent to which inherent biases in the National DNA Database may compromise the ability to identify 'causal' relationships between genetics markers and criminal behaviour and hence support misleading conclusions. Such scrutiny would need to balance any potential benefits from the research against the risks of increasing social stigmatisation and racial stereotyping, or a potential detrimental impact upon efforts to rehabilitate offenders** (paragraph 6.44).

36 Information provided by the NDNAD Strategy Board detailing requests that it has received for research access to the NDNAD and stored samples is superficial. In many instances, it is unclear what the research proposal actually led to. Requests for research with 'commercial' purposes will require particular scrutiny from the NDNAD Strategy Board, to ensure that research that primarily supports the development of a business opportunity does not gain approval unless fulfilling strict criteria. It is not clear that such strict criteria are currently

circumstances' criteria for removal of records from the NDNAD and other databases are too restrictive, and the Chief Constable's discretion too wide. If the current system remains and records are not automatically removed for those not convicted, in accordance with our earlier recommendations (paragraphs 10–12 and 20) we recommend that:

- **There should be public guidelines explaining how to apply to have records removed from police databases, and the grounds on which removal can be required.**
- **The police should be required to justify the need for retention in response to a request for removal of an individual's records (with a strong presumption in favour of removal in the case of minors, see paragraph 20).**
- **An independent body, along the lines of an administrative tribunal, should oversee requests from individuals to have their profiles removed from bioinformation databases. The tribunal would have to balance the rights of the individual against such factors as the seriousness of the offence, previous arrests, the outcome of the arrest, the likelihood of this individual re-offending, the danger to the public and any other special circumstances** (paragraph 7.37).

44 Although forensic biometric databases are not currently linked to each other in any sophisticated fashion, it is a stated aim for databases to be 'inter-operable' in the near future. The ethical implications of such databases could then be 'multiplied' by linking with other databases. The concerns, particularly about privacy, where access to one database may permit access to information across several databases, may be further compounded if linkage is envisaged between databases across different countries. **We recommend, on the basis of standard European data protection principles, a minimum set of safeguarding requirements to consider before allowing access to bioinformation databases to international law enforcement agencies, which would be:**

- **to ensure there is a sufficient level of data protection in all authorities/agencies that would receive information;**
- **to subject each request to adequate scrutiny as to merit and reasonableness and on a transparent basis;**
- **to agree the criteria for sharing data, for example only for the investigation of serious crimes or in special circumstances; and**
- **to share only as much information as is necessary to meet the request and only to those authorities or agencies which 'need to know'** (paragraph 7.42).

45 **In addition to the recommendations made in Chapter 6, we recommend, not only that there must be robust procedures for assessing applications for research access to the NDNAD and stored samples, but that there should also be a requirement to articulate publicly the basis upon which applications for any access to data stored on bioinformation databases will be considered and the precise purposes for which access will, and will not, be granted either to police or non-police agencies** (paragraph 7.32).

46 Exchanges of data internationally are currently made on a case-by-case basis, with no agreed framework for sharing data. Various initiatives are underway to facilitate exchanges while maintaining quality standards and adequate levels of protection for individual rights. There is no oversight body to monitor the international exchange of DNA profiles, or organisation that could make enquiries (and pursue complaints) on behalf of individuals whose data have been misused. There have also been recent proposals for a centralised database of fingerprints across the European Union, with an attendant obligation on each Member State to transfer details held by national police forces to a central authority.

47 The Prüm Treaty (2005) is a cooperation agreement for exchange of information between, currently, eleven European Union Member States.[5] It has been offered as a model for the entire European Union. The direct access provisions would not apply until the data protection elements of the Treaty have been adopted into national laws. **The threshold for holding DNA profiles on a forensic database is far lower in the United Kingdom than in any other Member State of the EU, and the proportion of the population included on the UK DNA Database is correspondingly far higher than in other EU countries. The Government should as a matter of urgency examine the implications of DNA exchanges for those on the UK NDNAD. The Government should insist on the inclusion in the Prüm Treaty of provisions to ensure that its operation is properly monitored. At the very least, the following is required:**

- **an obligation on national agencies to produce annual reports, including statistics, on the use of their powers under the Treaty; and**
- **an obligation on the European Commission to produce an overall evaluation of the operation of the Treaty, for submission to the European Council, the European Parliament and national parliaments, to see whether it needs amendment** (paragraph 7.52).

48 The current regulatory structure for bioinformation databases is not on a statutory footing and the legislative framework surrounding the forensic use of bioinformation is piecemeal and patchy. The regulatory architecture of forensic services is also currently in a state of flux in the United Kingdom.

49 **We recommend that there should be a statutory basis for the regulation of forensic databases and retained biological samples. A regulatory framework should be established with a clear statement of purpose and specific powers of oversight delegated to an appropriate independent body or official. This should include oversight of research and other access requests, for example for further testing of samples or familial searching and inferring ethnicity. We are pleased to see the establishment of an Ethics Group by the Home Office, with a remit to oversee the running and uses of the NDNAD, but its specific functions and powers must be more clearly, and publicly, articulated. Moreover, we consider that a longer-term view is required that considers the future possibilities and challenges that may come with increased access and linkage involving a range of forensic databases** (paragraph 7.55).

50 Throughout the Report we draw attention to the difficulty in assessing the impact of increasing police powers because of the poor quality or absence of official statistics (or conflicting statistics: see paragraphs 4.51–4.52). Moreover, on many vital issues such as requests to conduct research on databases and/or samples or general access provisions to the NDNAD, there is an absence of protocols or guidance. **We recommend a far greater commitment to openness and transparency and a greater availability of documents to public scrutiny. Where public access is denied for reasons of security and the administration of justice, this should be fully explained and justified. Efforts to improve the generation of data and statistics are welcomed, as are apparent efforts to increase the publication of data. These moves are still in their early stages, and their continuation is strongly supported** (paragraph 7.57).

5. Austria, Belgium, France, Germany, Luxembourg, the Netherlands, Spain, Finland, Italy, Portugal and Slovenia.

Chapter 1

Introduction

Introduction

The scope of this Report

1.1 In the policing of crime, state authorities increasingly rely on scientific technologies and, in particular, biotechnologies. Fingerprints, footprints and fragments of fibre have been used in the investigation and prosecution of crime since at least the end of the 19th Century. However, it is the development over the past two decades of the science and technology underpinning genetic 'fingerprinting' and now DNA profiling that has been the main reason for the dramatic increase in the use of bioinformation in the investigation and prosecution of crime. These biotechnologies are sometimes supplemented by other 'biometric' technologies that rely on the analysis of biological information such as iris scanning, voice analysis and gait analysis, and the comparison of facial images. Together, these resources have the potential to be combined to build 'multi-modal' identification systems. These might enable the police to link together several separate biometric and other databases. Platforms such as IDENT1 (which hosts the UK national fingerprint database, see paragraph 1.17) are already in place, which could greatly increase the power of these tools in the future by allowing linkage across databases and so facilitate the speed and efficacy of identification.

1.2 Since the implementation of the Police and Criminal Evidence Act 1984 (PACE) the powers of the police to take and retain fingerprints, DNA profiles and biological samples have been steadily increased, and until very recently the United Kingdom had the largest forensic DNA database in the world, the National DNA Database (NDNAD). (The US CODIS database has become slightly larger in terms of number of samples.) The increase in police powers has been achieved by piecemeal legislation. Although some proposed changes to PACE have been preceded by public consultation exercises and limited parliamentary debate, the lack of data on public attitudes to issues such as these was highlighted in 2005 by the House of Commons Select Committee on Science and Technology.[1] The establishment of the police DNA database was considered at the time an 'operational' decision and therefore was not considered to require public debate. Subsequent extensions to police powers, expansion of the NDNAD and further uses to which the NDNAD is now put have also lacked accompanying public discussion. There have been recent calls for a full public debate on the collection and use of bioinformation by the police, particularly on the uses of the NDNAD, and the Home Office has emphasised the need for clearly defined ethical standards:

> "In the application of science and technology, the [NDNAD] Strategy Group recognises the fundamental importance of ensuring that science and technology is used by the police only to enhance civil society. That is, in the sense of people's safe and secure enjoyment of their lives and property without intrusion that would breach their civil rights or scientific ethics."[2]

1.3 The aim of this Report is to provide an in-depth analysis to assist policy-makers and to raise public awareness of the issues. Our public consultation aroused widespread interest and we have benefited from written responses from organisations and members of the public, as well as from meetings with a number of key stakeholders (see Appendices 1 and 2). These reveal strong differences of opinion as to when fingerprints and biological samples should be taken and when these, and also DNA profiles, should be retained, and the uses to which potentially sensitive genetic information should be put. Our respondents fell into three broad groups:

- Those who wholeheartedly welcome the continued expansion of forensic bioinformation databases.

1. House of Commons Select Committee on Science and Technology (2005) *Forensic Science on Trial* (Norwich: The Stationery Office).
2. Home Office (2003) *Police Science and Technology Strategy 2003 to 2008* (Home Office Science Policy Unit), p14.

- Those who view the increase in police powers and use of bioinformation with deep suspicion.
- Those who take a middle position. They welcome the contribution that the new technologies and databases can make to crime control but they are concerned at the absence of effective governance. They want the utility of the databases to be maximised, but they also want their potentially harmful effects, such as threatening privacy, diminishing the requirement for informed consent, undermining social cohesion and engendering discriminatory practices, to be minimised. They seek safeguards against 'mission creep', particularly where the NDNAD is used for familial searching (searching the NDNAD for relatives of the person from whom DNA has been found in order to identify suspects), for making inferences about ethnicity from biological samples collected from crime scenes, and for research into criminal behaviour.

1.4 Those who are most enthusiastic about the forensic use of bioinformation place primary emphasis on the expectation that these technologies will contribute significantly to effective and efficient crime control by facilitating more speedy police investigations, as well as improving the rates at which crimes are detected and successfully prosecuted.[3] This emphasis on the contribution of bioinformation to crime control is usually accompanied by a number of detailed views, including some or all of the following:

- the police should have maximum access to DNA profiles from as many individuals as possible;
- consent should not be required to collect samples;
- the police should be able to retain all samples and profiles;
- all obtained profiles should be available for speculative searching on a database;
- current methods of DNA profiling are adequate;
- the levels of statistical certainty offered in support of DNA matches are adequate;
- DNA evidence is safe to secure conviction; and
- there is no reason to believe that enthusiasm for the use of DNA intelligence or evidence leads to miscarriages of justice.

1.5 However, other respondents are much less convinced by the benefits of using bioinformation to enhance and extend existing methods of crime control. These critics of the increasing use of DNA profiling and databasing have particular concerns with the ways in which scientific and technological advances need to be accommodated within 'due process' considerations that are central to contemporary criminal justice systems. This concern leads to a different series of ethical and operational preferences, including some or all of the following:

- the power of the police to obtain DNA profiles from individuals should be limited to those cases in which DNA evidence is relevant to the investigation;
- informed consent to DNA profiling should be regarded as foundational to the sampling of all persons, including criminal suspects;
- samples and profiles from those excluded from investigations should be destroyed;
- speculative searching of profiles on databases should be proscribed or at least time limited;
- current methods of DNA profiling should be regarded as inadequate and changed to increase their reliability;

3. Beyleveld D (1997) Ethical issues in the forensic applications of DNA analysis *Forensic Science International* 88: 3–15.

- the difficulties experienced by courts and jurors in evaluating the weight of forensic evidence should be recognised;
- 'match probabilities' (see paragraph 2.11) may be confusing and can result in unwarranted importance being attached to DNA evidence; and
- it is unacceptable to convict an individual using DNA evidence alone.

1.6 We put forward our own views and recommendations on these issues, not as the end of the debate, but hopefully as a contribution to the development of well-informed public engagement. We suggest means by which the public interest in crime control can be balanced in a proportionate way with other values (discussed in Chapter 3) such as liberty and autonomy, privacy, consent and equal treatment, and the legal protection of human rights and civil liberties. We have limited our investigation to two technologies: DNA profiling and fingerprinting. These are the two identification technologies most often relied upon in criminal investigations and criminal trials. Emergent biometric technologies such as iris identification, facial 'mapping' or voice recognition are yet to be accepted as fully reliable or useful for criminal investigation. However, pilot schemes and security systems are increasingly investing in the use of such technologies. Thus, although we concentrate on the two currently most robust technologies, we are not blind to other possibilities for the future.

1.7 We deal solely with issues raised by the forensic use of bioinformation in the criminal justice system. Ethical issues that arise with other 'forensic' uses of bioinformation, such as disputes about paternity or immigration, border security, or civil legal disputes fall outside our terms of reference. We do not consider the use of DNA or fingerprints to identify the dead or those missing after disasters: this use of bioinformation is generally seen as less controversial. Members of the public generally welcome the potential use of science for identifying loved ones. We have primarily focused on the legal situation in England and Wales, referring where appropriate to the separate legal provisions and databases in Scotland and Northern Ireland, where there are significant differences. We also make some comparisons with other European systems.

1.8 In this chapter we explain what is meant by 'bioinformation' and explain the technologies of fingerprinting and DNA profiling. We give a brief account of police powers to take biological samples and fingerprints, and of the NDNAD and the fingerprint database. In Chapter 2 we outline the scientific basis for the use and interpretation of bioinformation in forensic settings, including potential scientific developments. Chapter 3 outlines the ethical values and human rights that underpin our discussion. In Chapter 4 we consider the collection and subsequent uses of bioinformation during police investigations, and in Chapter 5 its use in criminal trials. Chapter 6 concentrates upon three particularly controversial uses: familial searching, inferring ethnicity and research into criminal behaviour, while Chapter 7 focuses upon governance and regulation of forensic databases and forensic services more broadly.

What is bioinformation?

1.9 Bioinformation may be derived from the analysis of a range of physical or biological characteristics of a person. It is most often used in efforts to identify individuals, or at least to differentiate individuals from each other. In particular, it is used:

- to ascertain whether somebody is the person they claim to be, or deny being; and
- to ascertain whether a person may have been in a particular place(s) or has been in contact with another person or object.

1.10 Bioinformation for determining whether a person is who they claim to be can involve, for example, the use of photographs, fingerprints or iris scans. The person in question is normally

> **Box 1.1: Current DNA profiling methodology**
>
> A DNA profile is obtained by:
>
> - extracting the DNA from a sample (blood, saliva, semen, sweat or other biological material);
> - measuring the amount of DNA obtained;
> - producing multiple copies of specific areas of DNA of interest (these correspond to the 'markers' referred to below); and
> - cataloguing the size of each marker in the particular individual from whom the DNA came.
>
> The technique currently used for DNA profiling in the United Kingdom is SGM Plus® (SGM+). It tests for ten 'markers', known as short tandem repeats (STRs), and a sex marker. STRs are short sequences of DNA that are repeated in tandem several times, and the number of repeats varies between individuals. The number of repeats is recorded and thus, a DNA profile consists of 20 two-digit numbers (each person has two copies of each marker, one inherited from each parent), and a sex indicator. The probability of a chance match between unrelated individuals using SGM+ is on average less than one in a billion (1,000,000,000). The discriminatory power of the analysis decreases for related individuals. SGM, a technique used before the introduction of SGM+, analysed six of the same markers plus the gender marker and had a lower discriminatory power. A proportion of the profiles on the NDNAD are based on SGM (22 per cent of criminal justice samples and 19 per cent of crime scene samples). When a current crime scene sample matches an SGM profile, the relevant biological sample is retrieved and the profile is upgraded to SGM+. A recent retrospective upgrade of 24,000 cases from SGM to SGM+ found that there were 3,600 cases where the profiles had originally matched using SGM, but no longer matched when using SGM+ profiling. To date, there have been no reports of chance matches between full SGM+ profiles. Chance matches are, however, more likely to arise:
>
> - with partial profiles;
> - between closely related individuals;
> - as the size of the NDNAD expands; and
> - between individuals within an isolated or inbred population.

present when these forms of bioinformation are used. Bioinformation for inferring whether a person may have been in a particular place, or in contact with another person or object may include photographs, images on CCTV cameras, fingerprints and DNA 'profiles' (see Box 1.1). Such 'trace biometrics' or 'trace bioinformation' can be used when the person is not physically present. This may or may not involve the use of a database, such as the police fingerprint database or the NDNAD.

1.11 Retrieved 'trace bioinformation' can also support inferences about what a person did when they were at the scene of a crime, such as handle a weapon or have sexual intercourse. However, the significance of such inferences depends on individual case circumstances, and, where the identity of the criminal remains disputed, it is likely that other evidence linking a suspect to a crime will be sought to support a prosecution. One of the issues discussed in this Report (see paragraphs 5.3 and 5.26) is whether a defendant could be convicted in circumstances where his or her only direct connection to the crime was a DNA match with a crime scene sample. Bioinformation used alone is unlikely to be sufficient to secure a conviction in criminal proceedings where the identity of the criminal is in dispute. An English court is likely to require additional evidence to be convinced that the suspect is the source of the bioinformation and the perpetrator of the offence, while in Scotland corroboration is a legal requirement.

DNA profiles and biological samples

1.12 It is of crucial importance to understand the distinction between a biological sample and a DNA profile. The former is the actual biological sample of body cells taken from a crime scene or from a suspect or a volunteer during an investigation. The latter is a string of numbers stored on the NDNAD (see paragraph 2.8). Generally, use and retention of a DNA profile raises far fewer ethical concerns than the use and retention of the biological sample. The DNA profile characterises only certain very restricted parts of a person's total DNA, and these areas of DNA have been selected largely because they provide no information beyond identifying the individual. Thus access to an individual's profile will not reveal anything of interest about that individual, beyond identification and gender (but see paragraph 2.20 for a small reservation concerning the sex indicator and Y chromosome markers). This will remain the case while the Single Generation Multiplex Plus (SGM+) profiling system is in use (see Chapter 2 for details), though with the rapid advancement of genetic analysis, and the decreasing cost of profiling greater sequences of DNA, it may not always remain so. The biological sample itself contains the whole genetic sequence of an individual, and is therefore far more sensitive in respect of privacy. Potentially, it might reveal personal, familial and health information, and perhaps even information about behavioural traits. There are a number of other profiling systems available, or in development, and there are moves to expand the amount of DNA that is currently profiled in order to make DNA profiles compatible internationally.

1.13 Another important distinction is made between, on the one hand, taking fingerprints and biological samples for direct use in investigating the offence for which the individual was arrested, and on the other hand, speculative searching against fingerprints and DNA profiles retained from previously unsolved crimes. While the initial taking of such bioinformation raises some ethical issues, it is the retention of this bioinformation in searchable databases that is of more serious ethical concern. In particular, permanent retention of biological samples and DNA profiles each require some further justification.

Fingerprints

1.14 The use of fingerprints by Scotland Yard dates back to the late 19th Century. Their use has been widely accepted for decades, their reliability and trusted status remaining intact in the face of recent critical scrutiny. Fingerprints serve two purposes within the criminal justice system:

- to establish identity and check that identity against an individual's prior criminal record; and
- to try to establish presence at a crime scene by comparison of 'latent' prints at the scene to stored fingerprints or fingerprints belonging to suspects.

It is this second purpose that is the most important for our purposes. However, recent policy on the use of fingerprints has stressed the utility of fingerprints for keeping track of individuals as they progress through the criminal justice system. For example, it is not unknown for individual A to try to impersonate individual B or for C and D to try to swap identities during the course of a police investigation or court proceedings.

1.15 Reforms to the legal provisions for fingerprinting have tackled the problems created when suspects give false details to the police. The previously time-consuming checking of a person's identity has been significantly speeded up with the introduction of 'LIVESCAN' digital fingerprint consoles at police stations. Since 2001, LIVESCAN terminals have automated the process of fingerprinting. The person places a hand on a glass platen, their fingerprints are captured electronically and then sent to IDENT1 for comparison, circumventing the problems associated with 'ink and roller' methods

1.16 The advent of DNA technology, with its discriminatory power and its lesser reliance upon human interpretation, has not diminished the use of fingerprints. Not only are they still used more frequently than DNA, but the development of mobile technology and of IDENT1, with its future capacity and capabilities, mean that fingerprints remain, and are likely to continue as, the dominant type of bioinformation in use in the criminal justice system.

The fingerprint database: IDENT1

1.17 The police currently hold over 6.5 million sets of fingerprints, stored in the 'National Tenprint

Collection' which is hosted on IDENT1, incorporating 20 per cent of the United Kingdom male population, and five per cent of the female population. There are also 1.2 million crime scene fingerprints on the 'Unidentified Marks Collection'. The law governing the taking of fingerprints mirrors that governing the taking of biological samples (see paragraphs 4.3–4.4). Fingerprints and DNA, together with photographs and shoe prints, may be taken at the same time. Similarly, members of the public may volunteer their prints for elimination purposes in criminal investigations.

1.18 IDENT1 is a 'platform' on which the police store databases such as the fingerprint database, a palm print database (PALMS) and a shoemark database. Other biometric databases may be added in time. IDENT1 is used to process 100,000 records of arrests every month. For the 12 months between February 2006 and January 2007, the average number of 'identifications' was 6,324 per month (see paragraphs 4.26–4.27). IDENT1 is used by all the police forces in England, Wales and Scotland as well as the Home Office Immigration and Nationality Directorate. In addition to 45 fingerprint bureaux in England and Wales, the British Transport Police, the Serious Organised Crime Agency (SOCA) and HM Revenue and Customs can access IDENT1. Approximately 1,200 police personnel have direct access to the fingerprint system.

1.19 Many questions about the collection, retention and use of bioinformation apply equally to fingerprints and DNA. Indeed, legislation has almost always linked the two by their joint inclusion in relevant sections of statutes, and since the redefinition of the mouth as a non-intimate area (see paragraph 4.9), fingerprints and other bioinformation have almost always been treated as equivalent matter. While some argue that DNA sampling is not qualitatively different from taking fingerprints, others claim that there are important distinctions between these two forms of bioinformation. In general, the taking and retention of DNA is seen as far more 'sensitive'. This is because fingerprints cannot reveal information beyond identity, whereas with DNA there is the possibility of deriving additional information about an individual by further analysis of their DNA, and about family relationships by comparing profiles. This special sensitivity surrounding DNA means that this Report pays particular attention to the uses of DNA within the criminal justice system. However, the potential 'multi-modal' future of IDENT1 – the ability to combine a series of different biometric databases to increase discriminatory identification power – may heighten concerns by increasing risks associated with the sharing of personal data (see Chapters 6 and 7).

Forensic DNA profiling

1.20 Deoxyribonucleic acid (DNA) is the chemical found in virtually every cell in our bodies. It affects our physical characteristics such as hair and eye colour and is unique to each individual (except identical twins). It also carries genetic information from one generation to the next. The identification of individuals using a technique known as 'genetic fingerprinting' was first used in 1985 during a major police investigation (the case of *Pitchfork*[4]). The potential of the technique, which was developed by Sir Alec Jeffreys, was soon realised, and legislation was introduced to facilitate its routine use. In the early 1990s the new genetic technique of DNA profiling superseded DNA fingerprinting (see Box 1.1).

The National DNA Database (NDNAD)

1.21 The NDNAD contains DNA profiles drawn from three primary sources:

- **criminal justice ('CJ arrestee') samples** – taken from those arrested for a recordable

4. See Walker C and Cram I (July 1990) DNA profiling and police powers *Criminal Law Review* 478–93, for a discussion of the case.

offence, without requiring their consent;

- **elimination samples** – taken from victims and consenting volunteers to establish that they can be excluded from further investigation, or to identify the source of profiles left innocently at a crime scene; and
- **crime scene samples** – DNA found at a crime scene.

Most DNA profiles on the NDNAD have been taken from persons arrested by the police. A smaller number are from individuals who have witnessed a crime or who have consented to a biological sample being taken in order to eliminate them from a criminal investigation ('elimination samples'). These two categories are not distinguished once loaded onto the NDNAD and are both known as 'subject samples'. Additional DNA profiles have been secured through analysis of trace biological material deposited at scenes of crime by unidentified individuals. All subject samples are entered onto the NDNAD, unless donated by volunteers who have not consented to their DNA profile being permanently entered on the NDNAD. The DNA profile then forms part of that individual's electronic criminal justice record (see Box 1.3). (An individual providing an elimination subject sample will not have an arrest summons number recorded.)

1.22 As we have said, the United Kingdom has for many years had the largest forensic DNA database in the world, incorporating approximately six per cent of the UK population. The FBI's 'CODIS' database in the USA has recently become the world's largest DNA database, but although this is larger in size, it covers a far smaller proportion of the whole population: approximately 0.5 per cent.[5] The next largest forensic DNA database, in terms of coverage of the population, is in Austria, with one per cent of the population on its DNA database. At the end of March 2007, the UK NDNAD held approximately four million DNA profiles from subject samples and over 264,000 profiles from crime scene samples. Over 25,000 of the subject samples were from volunteers. In 2005–6, 715,239 subject sample profiles and 68,774 crime stain profiles were added to the NDNAD. It is estimated that approximately 13.7 per cent of subject samples are 'replicates', so the samples do not represent four million different individuals.[6] Replication may occur where an individual has been arrested on more than one occasion, and, having given a false name, has a further biological sample taken.[7]

1.23 No single legislative instrument or Act of Parliament established the NDNAD or the police powers to take and retain biological samples from citizens. Instead, the growing collection, storage and use of DNA and biological samples has been facilitated piecemeal by successive amendments to legislation, especially amendments to the Police and Criminal Evidence Act (PACE) of England and Wales 1984. Since the enactment of the Criminal Justice Act 2003, the police have been permitted to take fingerprints and biological samples from any individual arrested for a recordable offence, without their consent, whether or not DNA or fingerprints are relevant to the crime being investigated. This bioinformation is retained indefinitely on IDENT1 and the NDNAD databases, irrespective of whether the person is charged or convicted of an offence. These fingerprints and DNA profiles are then permanently available for comparison with others from individuals and crime scenes. Victims and witnesses might also be asked to submit their fingerprints and biological samples for elimination purposes.

1.24 While the number of people being fingerprinted and having biological samples taken has increased dramatically, this still amounts to only a proportion of those arrested. In the year 2004–5, over 1.3 million people were arrested[8] and 34.6 per cent of those arrested had biological samples taken and profiled. At present the person must have been arrested for a

5. As of April 2007, the profile composition of CODIS (the US National DNA Index System) is as follows: total number of profiles: 4,630,929 (4,457,313 from convicted offenders) and 173,616 'crime scene' DNA profiles.

6. House of Commons, Hansard, 10 May 2007, column 431W.

7. There are also records held for almost 1,400 identical twins, and two sets of triplets.

8. Twenty-five per cent of these were aged under 17, whereas 40 per cent were under 21.

Box 1.2: Offence categories

Arrestable offences: The distinctions between 'non-arrestable', 'arrestable' and 'serious arrestable' offences were abolished in England and Wales with the passing of the Serious Organised Crime and Police Act 2005. Thus, the power of arrest now applies to all offences, however minor. Police officers can arrest someone who is about to commit an offence, is in the act of committing an offence, or where the officer has reasonable grounds for suspecting either of these is the case, or they have reasonable grounds to suspect an individual has committed an offence. Section 110 of the Act provides that such powers must only be exercised where a constable has reasonable grounds for believing that arrest is 'necessary'. PACE Code G gives guidance, stating for example that an arrest may be necessary if there are reasonable grounds to believe someone has made statements 'which cannot be readily verified', or may intimidate or contact witnesses.

Recordable offences: All offences that carry the possibility of a custodial sentence are recordable (or 'notifiable'), plus 52 other, non-imprisonable offences specified in the Schedule to the National Police Records (Recordable Offences) (Amendment) Regulations 2005 (SI 2005/3106). Regulations made before 1997 had listed five non-imprisonable offences as recordable: loitering or soliciting for purposes of prostitution; improper use of public telecommunications system; tampering with vehicles; sending letters, etc. with intent to cause distress or anxiety; and having an article with a blade or point in public place. In 1997, a further 42 offences were added to the list and then in 2000, another five offences were added, and the provisions consolidated. The 2003 Amendment Regulations added offences of taxi touting, begging and persistent begging to the list.

Non-recordable offences: These include all other offences that do not attract a possible custodial sentence, and are not included in the list of recordable offences. These are 'minor' offences such as littering, minor public order offences and minor traffic offences. However, if the Home Office proposals of March 2007 were to be implemented, then all offences could become 'recordable' in the sense that a report of these arrestees would necessitate the creation of a 'record' of that arrest and the related offence.

recordable offence (see Box 1.2) before they can be fingerprinted and have a biological sample taken (nearly all offences are recordable). However, Home Office proposals announced in March 2007 suggest that this restriction may be lifted, with the police permitted to take fingerprints and biological samples from any arrestee, regardless of offence. This would extend sampling to people who have been arrested on suspicion of minor offences, such as minor traffic offences or littering. There are some two million arrests made each year (many of the same individuals), with upwards of 25 per cent of the male population and seven per cent of the female population of England and Wales arrested during their lifetime. With this potential further extension of police sampling powers, the NDNAD could expand dramatically, soon encompassing a fifth or more of the population. We comment upon these proposals later in this Report (see paragraphs 4.21–4.23).

1.25 There are a variety of legal positions taken across continental Europe and internationally about the taking and retention of bioinformation from citizens. These are set out in Box 4.3.

Scotland

1.26 The situation in Scotland, which has a separate legal system and policing tradition, differs from that in England and Wales.[9] Whereas it was once necessary to obtain the authorisation of a police inspector to take mouth swabs, these can now be taken on arrest by a police constable. However, the samples and resulting profiles must be destroyed if the individual is not convicted or is granted an absolute discharge. A recent qualification provides that biological samples and profiles may be retained for three years, if the arrestee is suspected of certain sexual or violent offences[10] even if a person is not convicted.[11] Thereafter, samples and information should be destroyed unless a Chief Constable applies to a Sheriff for a two-year extension. The onus is on the police to show reasonable grounds for retention.[12] Another distinguishing feature of the Scottish position is that while volunteer samples can be retained with consent as in England, this consent can be withdrawn at any time, requiring destruction of the relevant sample and related

9. The principal legislation is the Criminal Procedure (Scotland) Act 1995, as amended by the Criminal Justice (Scotland) Act 2003 and the Police, Public Order and Criminal Justice (Scotland) Act 2006.

10. Including rape, indecent assault and lewd and libidinous behaviour; murder, assault and reckless conduct causing actual injury.

11. S.83 of the 2006 Act, adding S.18A to the 1995 Act.

12. This application must be within three months of the due destruction date. The law does not preclude repeat requests for further extensions of two years. A final appeal is possible to a Sheriff Principal.

information.[13] The Scottish DNA Database, situated within Tayside Police headquarters, holds in excess of 200,000 DNA profiles. During 2005–6, 4,591 crime scene samples were received, and 68 per cent of these matched with subject samples on the local database. The remaining 32 per cent of crime scene samples were then exported to the UK NDNAD.

Northern Ireland

1.27 The Northern Ireland DNA Database operates under different legislation from that in England, Wales and Scotland,[14] but the law mirrors that of England and Wales. DNA may be taken without consent from anyone charged with a recordable offence, aged ten or above, who is taken into police custody. DNA profiles are entered on the Northern Ireland DNA Database (NIDNAD) and biological samples are stored by the Forensic Science Northern Ireland (FSNI) laboratory, which also acts as the Custodian (see paragraph 1.30) of the NIDNAD.[15] The size of the NIDNAD has risen from 17,000 in 2000 to 39,055 in 2007 (this figure is broken down as: 3,355 samples taken from children (those aged under 18) and 35,700 samples taken from adults (those aged 18 and over)).[16]

1.28 Since July 2005, the NIDNAD has submitted its DNA profiles to the UK NDNAD, under a 2006/07 PSNI-FSNI (Police Service of Northern Ireland) agreement, which also allows 'familial' searching (see paragraphs 6.6–6.11) using the Database. The law in Northern Ireland allows permanent retention of all profiles and samples taken from arrested individuals. However, it is not yet police policy in Northern Ireland to use their full sampling and retention powers and the policy of the police is to remove profiles from the NIDNAD if an individual is acquitted or removed from suspicion. These profiles are not then uploaded onto UK NDNAD.[17] While this is the stated policy, the retention of DNA in Northern Ireland in cases where no conviction or caution has resulted is in fact becoming widespread. The retention of DNA from children has particularly attracted attention, with DNA held on approximately 3,000 young people under the age of 18, of whom 1,119 have no convictions or cautions.[18]

Access to the UK NDNAD

1.29 A number of agencies have access to the NDNAD, including:

- Members of the NDNAD Custodian Unit in the Home Office who have responsibility for maintaining the integrity and oversight of the NDNAD (18 staff members).[19]
- Members of the Forensic Science Service Ltd. who have responsibility for providing NDNAD operational services, which includes loading DNA profiles onto the NDNAD to search for matches and reporting these back to police forces (31 staff members).

1.30 There are at present seven organisations accredited by the Custodian,[20] (three of which are private companies, the rest being police or public sector laboratories: see paragraph 7.11) and authorised to generate DNA profiles from subject samples or crime scenes and have

13. S.56 of the 2003 Act.
14. The authority arises from the Police and Criminal Evidence (Northern Ireland) Order 1989, as amended by the Police (Amendment) (Northern Ireland) Order 1995 and the Criminal Justice (Northern Ireland) Order 2004.
15. Forensic Science Northern Ireland (2006) *Annual Report 2005/06*.
16. Paul Goggins MP, Hansard, 15 June 2007, column 1395W.
17. Forensic Science Northern Ireland (2006) *Annual Report 2005/06*.
18. Statewatch (2006) Northern Ireland: DNA data held on 1,119 innocent children, available at: http://www.statewatch.org/news/2006/oct/13ni-dna-children.htm, accessed on: 2 July 2007.
19. Joan Ryan, for the Home Office, Hansard, 9 May 2006, column 199W.
20. A Home Office unit responsible for setting the expected Standards of Performance for forensic science laboratories that provide DNA profiles for the NDNAD and ensuring that these are achieved and maintained. This unit is also responsible for overseeing delivery of the NDNAD operations contract by the Forensic Science Service.

them uploaded onto the NDNAD by the Forensic Science Service.[21] International law enforcement agencies may request permission to search the NDNAD (although there remain problems of compatibility of the NDNAD with databases of other countries) and transfer of data can be arranged, usually via Europol or Interpol (see paragraphs 7.42–7.53).

Box 1.3: What information is stored on the NDNAD?

The NDNAD contains electronic records relating to DNA profiles generated from biological samples. The DNA profiles can be generated from analysis of material from crime scenes, submitted to the NDNAD with accompanying information about the offences and locations with which they are associated. DNA profiles are also generated from 'subject samples' taken from individuals. The biological samples are kept in storage, while the electronic record on the NDNAD contains the following information:

1 an arrest summons number (ASN) providing a link to the record on the Police National Computer (PNC), which contains the person's criminal record and any police intelligence information;[22]

2 information about the police force that collected the sample of DNA;

3 the person's name, date of birth, ethnic appearance (as defined by the police) and their gender;

4 details of the type of biological sample from which the DNA is taken (blood, semen, saliva, etc.);

5 the type of DNA test used;

6 the DNA profile (a string of 20, two-digit numbers and a sex indicator);

7 a unique bar-code reference number (linking to the location of the stored biological sample).

21. These organisations are: The Forensic Science Service Ltd., LGC Ltd., Orchid Cellmark Ltd., Tayside Police Forensic Science Laboratory, Forensic Science Northern Ireland, Strathclyde Police Forensic Science Laboratory, and Lothian and Borders Police Forensic Science Laboratory. Further organisations are currently seeking accreditation.

22. If volunteers have consented to their profile being entered onto the database, a similar record will be generated but will not include an arrest summons number.

Chapter 2

The interpretation of bioinformation

The interpretation of bioinformation

Introduction

2.1 This chapter examines fingerprinting and the science underlying DNA profiling, and considers how they are developing. Early problems with interpretation and reliability appear to have been overcome, but new procedures that push techniques to their limits raise questions about the accuracy, reliability and interpretation of these technologies. Widespread automation using computers and robots has lessened reliance upon humans, but with both fingerprints and DNA, human fallibility may still result in flaws even if the most robust scientific techniques are used.

Fingerprint comparison

2.2 The genesis of the 'science' of dactyloscopy – commonly known as 'fingerprinting' – has been well documented, if remaining disputed.[1] Although DNA is hailed as the 'gold standard' of identification techniques, the more humble fingerprint retains its status as the most commonly used method of identification and is a cornerstone of forensic crime scene investigation. Despite controversy over the standard required before a 'match' can be declared, fingerprint evidence generally remains unassailable in the criminal courts as a unique identifier. However, disputes can and do arise about methods of collection or negligent interpretation, and there have been several criminal cases where fingerprint evidence has proven flawed (see Box 2.1).

2.3 Finger skin is made of friction ridges, with pores (sweat glands). Friction ridges are created

Box 2.1: Fingerprint flaws?

- Mr Chiori was arrested and charged with burglary after a fingerprint expert claimed 'no doubt' about a match between Chiori's fingerprints with those at a crime scene, this being the only evidence. Two independent experts found the match to be wrong. At trial, the prosecution explained that their expert had made an error of judgment and the case against Chiori would not be pursued. The defence expert claimed that there was evidence of gross negligence and incompetence on the part of the Metropolitan Police Fingerprint Bureau (although without malicious intent). Chiori sought compensation at the European Court of Human Rights.[2] This was unsuccessful as it was ruled that police and fingerprint officers were immune from prosecution.
- In 1998, Scottish police officer Shirley McKie was tried and convicted of perjury for testifying that a fingerprint on a doorframe at a murder scene was not hers. Four fingerprint experts testified to a match with McKie, while two American experts gave contrary testimony. McKie's conviction was overturned. Controversy continues over how the erroneous 'match' got through the Scottish Criminal Records Office procedures. Shirley McKie recently received £750,000 compensation.[3]
- In the United States of America, an attorney from Oregon, Brandon Mayfield, was arrested for involvement in the Madrid train bombings after a fingerprint 'match' by the Federal Bureau of Investigation (FBI). The FBI reported a match against one of 20 fingerprint candidates returned by their automated fingerprint database. The FBI called the match '100 per cent positive' and 'absolutely incontrovertible'. The Spanish National Police examiners concluded the prints did not match Mayfield. The FBI subsequently acknowledged the error, and Mayfield was released after two weeks in custody. In January 2006, the US Justice Department found the misidentification was due to misapplication of methodology by examiners and ordered the FBI pay Mayfield US$2 million in compensation.[4]
- Research by Dr Itiel Dror of the University of Southampton demonstrates that the context in which an examiner undertakes a fingerprint comparison can influence the expert's conclusions.[5] He concludes that fingerprint experts can be influenced by the context in which they are asked to evaluate the evidence (particularly the emotional context) and that the same expert can come to different conclusions about the same fingerprint when asked to evaluate the match on successive occasions without the expert knowing of his or her earlier conclusion.

1. For example, see Beavan C (2003) *Fingerprints* (London: Fourth Estate) and Cole S (2001) *Suspect Identities* (Massachusetts: Harvard University Press).
2. *Chiori v UK* (1999) ECHR App. No. 44926/98.
3. See www.shirleymckie.com for details.
4. Eggen D (2006) US settles suit filed by Ore. Lawyer: $2 million will be paid for wrongful arrest after Madrid attack *Washington Post*, 30 November, pA03.
5. Dror IE and Charlton D (2006) Why experts make errors *Journal of Forensic Identification* **56:** 600–16.

during foetal development and only the general shape is genetically defined. Fingerprint patterns then vary from person to person (including identical twins) and no two people have been found with the same fingerprints. Fingerprints also remain unchanged throughout life. Identification by fingerprints relies on the matching of patterns and the detection of certain ridge characteristics, also known as Galton details (after Sir Francis Galton who originated the technique). These points of identity, or minutiae, and the comparison of the relative positions of these minutiae points with a reference print (either inked impression of a suspect's print or digital representation), are the basis of fingerprint comparison. Identification points consist of points such as bifurcations, ending ridges, and islands (see Figure 2.1). A single fingerprint may have as many as 100 or more identification points.

Figure 2.1: Image of a fingerprint with some ridge characteristics identified

Image from http://perso.orange.fr/fingerchip/biometrics/types/fingerprint.htm

2.4 When fingerprints were first used, there were no set criteria to determine a 'match'. Practitioners originally argued that finding 12 similar ridge characteristics was the point at which to declare a match. However, in 1924, New Scotland Yard adopted a 16-point standard, and in 1953 it was agreed at a national policy level that this would become the common national approach. Other countries operate with 8, 10 or 12 points or have no numerical standard. In 1988, the Home Office and the Association of Chief Police Officers (ACPO) concluded that there was no scientific basis for the retention of the numerical standard. In 1995, a Home Office report stated that fingerprinting: "was not an exact science" but involved judgment.[6] A target was set that by 2000, the numerical approach would be superseded. In 1999, this target was endorsed by *R v Buckley*,[7] where the courts set down new guidance on the admission of fingerprint evidence (see Chapter 5). On 11 June 2001, national guidance was provided to all fingerprint bureaux by ACPO that the 16-point standard be replaced by a non-numerical standard which has 'objective criteria'.[8] This guidance makes clear that whether or not a fingerprint 'match' has been found is a matter of opinion by a fingerprint expert, and cannot be presented as a fact.

6. Evett IW and Williams RL (1995) *A Review of the Sixteen Point Fingerprint Standard In England and Wales* (London: Home Office), p11.
7. *R v Buckley* (1999) 143 SJ LB 159.
8. Typically, the finding of various points of similarity in ridge patterns. Lord Rooker, House of Lords, Hansard, 25 February 2002, column 2701.

Forensic DNA profiling

How is DNA bioinformation obtained?

2.5 The police can obtain a biological sample (containing DNA) either directly from a suspect, or from a consenting victim or volunteer (a 'subject sample'), or from a crime scene or exhibit (for example, clothing, footwear or a weapon). Bar-coded samples are received by the processing laboratory and put through a standard process to yield a few drops of water containing DNA in a bar-coded plastic tube. Any of the physical biological sample and extracted DNA that is not used up in the laboratory is stored indefinitely (the 'biological sample').

2.6 Subject samples are normally obtained by brushing the inside of a person's cheek with an instrument like a small toothbrush (a 'buccal swab'). This should yield an ample quantity of good quality DNA. Crime scene stains are much more variable. Bloodstains are the best source, although very small spots (1 mm or less in size) can be difficult. Other frequently used sources include cigarette ends, chewing gum, saliva obtained from drinking vessels, scarves, balaclavas, etc., hair and semen (Table 2.1 shows the proportions and success rates in obtaining a profile suitable for loading on to the NDNAD from various types of crime scene stains). Hard surfaces with which the offender is thought to have had skin contact can be swabbed and may yield minute amounts of DNA even when no stain is visible.

Table 2.1: The proportions and success rates in obtaining a profile suitable for loading on to the NDNAD from various types of crime scene stains, July–September 2005.

Relative recovery and profiling rates for DNA sources, July–September 2005

DNA Group	Percentage of Total Samples Processed	Percentage of Samples for Loading on NDNADB
Blood	26.1	86.1
Cigarette ends	24.0	73.5
Saliva	27.1	37.2
Chewing gum	0.9	71.2
Hair	1.1	18.1
Semen	5.2	92.1
Cellular	15.6	12.4

Source: Bond JW (2007) Value of DNA evidence in detecting crime *Journal of Forensic Sciences* **52:** 128–36. Reprinted with permission from Blackwell Publishing.

2.7 A small portion of the extracted DNA is used to obtain a DNA profile. A standard laboratory technique (the polymerase chain reaction, or PCR) is used to make millions of copies of specific parts of the original DNA, the 'markers'. These markers consist of repeated short sequences of DNA that vary in length between different people. The current standard profiling technique in the United Kingdom, SGM+, uses ten markers of a type called short tandem repeats (STRs) (see Box 1.1 and Appendix 4 for further details).

2.8 Each cell of a person contains two copies (alleles) of each marker, one from the father and one from the mother. These differ in various ways between individuals. The PCR product contains millions of copies of each marker in the SGM+ set. This fluid is put into a machine that plots the length of each marker sequence in the form of peaks on a graph (Figure 2.2). The graph is reviewed by a scientist to check its quality, completeness and any ambiguity. The profile is then entered on to the NDNAD. The profile stored on the NDNAD consists of a series of 20 numbers, recording the size of each allele of each marker, plus a sex indicator, together with other information such as name and date of birth (see Box 1.3).

Figure 2.2: A DNA profile as obtained in the laboratory

The figure shows an electropherogram of the SGM+ profile from a male. The numbers beneath the peaks indicate the allele sizes in repeat units. The profile stored on the NDNAD consists of only these numbers. The diagram is included for illustrative purposes only.

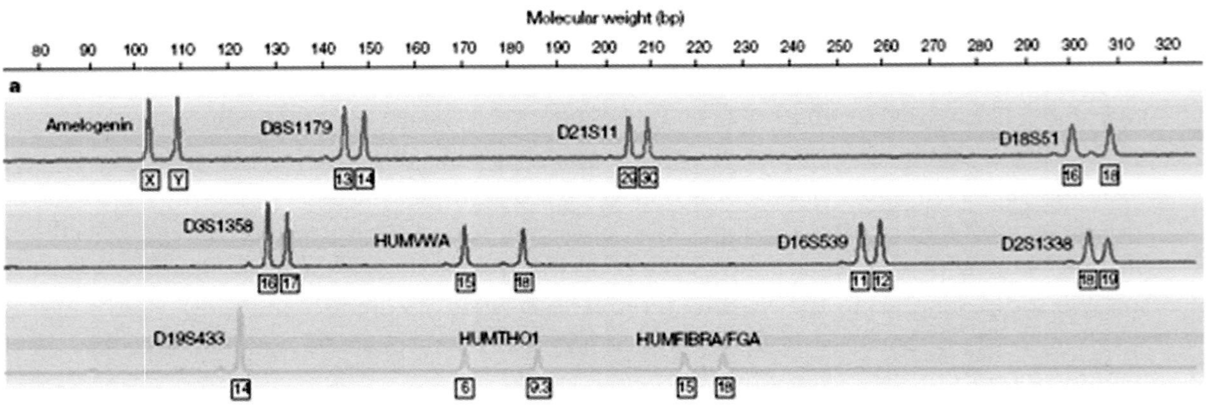

Source: Jobling MA and Gill P (2004) Encoded evidence: DNA in forensic science *Nature Reviews Genetics* **5**: 739–51. Reprinted by permission from Macmillan Publishers Ltd: copyright 2004.

How has the science of DNA profiling developed?

2.9 The 'DNA fingerprinting' method was developed by Sir Alec Jeffreys in 1984. The original DNA fingerprints consisted of a pattern of bands rather like a bar-code. For judging a match, bands were assigned to arbitrarily defined 'bins'. Each bin either contained a band or did not contain a band. The crime scene and subject samples were compared for the presence or absence of a band in each bin. The rarity, or match probability, was calculated from a database showing the probability that a random biological sample would have a band in any particular bin. This method, involving expert judgment of arbitrary patterns, is analogous to the way fingerprints are classified and compared.

2.10 This method has now been superseded by a quicker and more sensitive laboratory technique which is applicable to even very small and relatively degraded biological samples. Using 'STR profiles' allows a much more analytical and theoretically grounded approach to matching. Each marker can be assigned to a specific STR and characterised by its precise size. Sizes are not continuously variable, but consist of integer numbers of DNA units. Databases show the frequency of each size of allele of each STR in a variety of populations.

2.11 The match probability of a profile is the probability that an unrelated individual would have the same profile by random chance. It is calculated by multiplying together the chance of a match for each individual peak on the graph (see Appendix 4 for a discussion of this procedure). It depends on how common or rare each particular variant is in the population. For SGM+, match probability is normally much less than 1 in 1 billion (1,000,000,000). However, the chance of a match with a relative is much higher. Identical twins have identical profiles.

2.12 If requested, laboratories will 'type' a sample for a series of additional markers. This could be with the purpose of increasing the discriminating power of a profile or as an aid to familial searching (see paragraphs 2.15–2.16). Some of the most common additional analyses are detailed in Box 2.2.

Box 2.2: Additional DNA analysis techniques

Y-chromosome markers (Y-short tandem repeats (Y-STRs) or Y-single nucleotide polymorphisms (Y-SNPs)): The Y chromosome is present only in males. A man's specific combination of sequences on the Y chromosome is normally inherited unchanged from his father. The combination ('haplotype') can help with identification, and can provide probabilistic information about the geographical origin of somebody's male ancestors.

Variants in mitochondrial DNA (mtDNA): Unlike Y-chromosome variants, this small component of the DNA (which is not in the chromosomes but contained in a distinct component of each cell) is present in people of both sexes, but is inherited exclusively from the mother. Again, the particular combination of variants in mitochondrial DNA is normally inherited unchanged from an individual's mother, and may assist with identification or provide probabilistic information about ancestry, this time of the maternal ancestors. Additionally, because a single cell contains many copies of the mtDNA, this DNA can sometimes be analysed in samples that are too small or degraded to allow standard profiling. Y-chromosome and mtDNA data do not fit the template of standard NDNAD records, and we have not been able to establish whether, and if so where and how, this information is databased.

Low copy number (LCN) analysis: The standard profiling technique is designed to be reliable for amounts of DNA equivalent to the content of 20 cells. The LCN method aims to produce SGM+ profiles from still smaller amounts of DNA.[9] The standard SGM+ PCR reaction, which produces many copies of each marker allele, is run for longer with the aim of producing analysable numbers of copies from less starting material. LCN has allowed some high-profile 'cold' cases to be solved but the results are much more open to interpretation than profiles obtained on larger samples (see paragraphs 2.30–2.31). Usually several independent replicates of the LCN reaction are performed, and alleles are only reported if they appear in more than one replicate.

Pendulum: One of several computer programs for assisting the interpretation of mixed samples (from more than one person). Pendulum works by considering all possible solutions, identifying the most self-consistent ones and calculating the statistical support for each possible interpretation. It does not perform the interpretation, but helps the reporting officer form an expert opinion.

2.13 Crime scene stains are often much more difficult to analyse than subject samples. This is for one or more of three reasons:

- They may contain the DNA of several people (mixed samples).
- They may yield extremely small amounts of DNA. This challenges the technical limits of the PCR process, and increases the problems caused by possible contamination with extraneous DNA.
- The DNA may be fragmented into small pieces ('degraded') as a result of exposure to environmental agents. This can cause difficulties with the PCR process. Such difficulties may result in the profiling process producing a 'partial profile', that is a profile without the full set of ten markers.

2.14 Technical developments to assist with these problems include computer programs to help distinguish the individual profiles in a mixed sample, variants of the PCR process to analyse very small samples (e.g. the DNA low copy number (LCN) method used by the Forensic Science Service) and special markers (mini-STRs) that can be typed from highly degraded samples. As discussed below, interpretation of results obtained from such samples can be controversial.

What other uses may be made of DNA?

Familial searching

2.15 In difficult criminal investigations where a suspect cannot be identified, the police may request that 'near misses' – where there may 'nearly' be a match between DNA profiles – are further explored. If a crime scene profile does not completely match any subject profile on the NDNAD, it is possible to see if any subject profile could be from a relative of the person who deposited the crime scene sample. Familial searching is the process of comparing a DNA profile from a crime scene with subject profiles stored on the NDNAD, and prioritising them in terms of

9. The Forensic Science Service (2005) *DNA Low Copy Number*, available at: www.forensic.gov.uk/forensic_t/inside/news/fact_sheets.htm, accessed on: 2 July 2007.

'closeness' to a match. Parents and children always share one allele of each marker. For the ten SGM+ markers, there would be 1,024 possible combinations of shared alleles. For siblings (brothers and sisters) a search is simply made for profiles that share an unexpectedly large proportion of sequences, particularly very unusual sequences, with the crime scene sample. Unrelated individuals share on average six of the 20 SGM+ alleles in a profile, just by chance, whereas siblings share on average 13–14 alleles, but in each case there is a wide distribution around these averages.[10] Currently a search of the NDNAD for profiles that share alleles with a crime scene sample might identify ten profiles that share 16 alleles, 20–30 profiles that share 15, several hundred that share 14, and several thousand that share 13 alleles.

2.16 The size of this pool must be limited geographically and/or by other means to produce a useful short-list. One way of reducing the list would be to 'type' both the crime scene stain and all retained subject samples on the shortlist for mitochondrial and/or Y-chromosome variants (depending on the type of relationship assumed). Eventually a person identified through familial searching would be asked to provide a biological sample, and would be identified as a suspect or eliminated from the enquiry depending whether this sample then matched the crime scene profile. The familial search results would not form part of the evidence presented in any prosecution. Nevertheless, there was considerable concern among respondents to our consultation about the potential of familial searching to be intrusive or improperly reveal family secrets. This is addressed in Chapter 6.

Ethnic inferences

2.17 All alleles of the SGM+ markers can be found in all ethnic groups, but particular alleles are more or less frequent in different groups. The particular combination of alleles in an SGM+ profile can be used to assess the most likely ethnic origin of the donor. These calculations are based upon research that was completed by the Forensic Science Service, using a sample of DNA profiles taken from the NDNAD. Such an 'ethnic inference' is occasionally made from a crime scene stain in the hope of narrowing the pool of suspects (i.e. to indicate that the suspect is likely to have a particular ethnic appearance). A more detailed inference could be made by analysing the actual DNA rather than the profile, using markers chosen because the allele frequency varies considerably between groups ('ancestry informative markers'). Any ethnic inference may be more or less specific, but it is unlikely ever to be unambiguous. Global mobility and ethnic mixing limit the value of such inferences. In the light of the social factors and policing practices that lead to a disproportionate number of people from black and ethnic minority groups being stopped, searched and arrested by the police, and hence having their DNA profiles recorded on the NDNAD, there are concerns that inferring ethnic identity from biological samples risks reinforcing racist views of propensity to criminality. These issues are discussed in Chapter 6.

A DNA photofit?

2.18 In principle, other physical characteristics might be predictable by more extensive analysis of the biological sample (but not of the DNA profile). The striking physical similarity of identical twins demonstrates that a person's DNA sequence has a very significant influence upon their general physical appearance. Given sufficient scientific knowledge, and a sufficiently complete DNA analysis, a photo-fit picture of the suspect could in theory be generated from a crime scene sample.[11] This is not currently anywhere near possible. Most human characteristics, even if they are partly determined by our DNA sequence, depend on the combined effects of many variables, each of which has only a small effect. It has proved extremely difficult to predict

10. Information provided by Richard Pinchin, Forensic Intelligence Bureau, 16 February 2007.

11. Although this would also rely on assumptions being made about the environment in which a person has been brought up (nutrition during childhood, childhood diseases, etc.).

observable human characteristics from analysis of DNA, except for certain genetic diseases that affect only a small proportion of the population. Research is continuing, including into the possibilities of deriving useful descriptive information from crime scene samples. Past experience suggests that progress is likely to be slow and unspectacular. The following deductions have been widely discussed:

- **Hair colour:** The FSS claims to be able to identify 84 per cent of redheads by analysis of the sequence of the *MC1R* gene. Other hair colours are not readily predictable. Of course, any such test simply provides information on genetic hair colour - it could not tell if somebody is bald or has dyed hair.
- **Eye colour:** Several genes have been identified that contribute to determining eye colour, which may allow limited probabilistic predictions.[12]
- **Skin colour:** This is known to be determined by a series of different genes, some of which have been specifically identified. The ethnic inferences described above would give some suggestions about possible skin colour.

Surnames

2.19 Since a man's Y chromosome and, often in the United Kingdom, his surname are both inherited down the male line, there is some correlation between Y-chromosome marker haplotypes and surnames of individuals born in the UK. For uncommon surnames the correlation might be sufficiently tight to help narrow a pool of suspects. The accuracy of surname inferences is untested in practice, but has been supported in a pilot study, at least for unusual surnames.[13] Such inferences would of course fail if a person's surname did not reflect his true biological paternity as in the case of children adopted, not given their father's surname or not the biological offspring of their 'social' father.[14]

Health-related information

2.20 It is very unlikely that present forensic analysis of crime scene stains could yield health-related information about the donor, nor is it obvious what purpose would be served by attempting to obtain such information. The DNA profiles stored on the NDNAD do not predict any characteristics of a person, apart from their sex. We note, however, that the sex test that is part of the standard SGM+ profile will reveal rare individuals whose chromosomal sex does not match their physical sex or social gender, while testing Y-chromosome markers has the potential to inadvertently reveal certain deletions that can cause infertility in rare individuals. Either test might reveal sex chromosome abnormalities. Such inadvertent discoveries are perhaps analogous to the occasional inadvertent discovery of wrong paternity in the course of clinical genetic testing. General practice among clinical geneticists in the United Kingdom is not to inform the subject.

2.21 Any deliberate attempt to uncover health-related data would be contrary to the Council of Europe's Recommendation on the Protection of Medical Data, Principle 4.8 of which states for forensic DNA analysis that: "The data should only be used to establish whether there is a genetic link in the framework of adducing evidence, to prevent a real danger or to suppress a specific criminal offence. In no case should they be used to determine other characteristics which may be linked genetically."[15] (See Appendix 3.)

12. Duffy DL, Montgomery GW, Chen W et al. (2007) A three-single-nucleotide polymorphism haplotype in intron 1 of OCA2 explains most human eye-color variation *American Journal of Human Genetics* **80:** 241–52.
13. King TE, Ballereau SJ, Schürer K and Jobling MA (2006) Genetic signatures of coancestry within surnames *Current Biology* **16:** 384–8.
14. Jobling M (2001) In the name of the father: surnames and genetics *Trends in Genetics* **17**: 353–7.
15. Council of Europe (1997) Recommendation R (97) 5 on the Protection of Medical Data.

Future scientific developments

2.22 Whether there is any benefit in adding more markers to the standard SGM+ set is debatable. Further markers can always be analysed in particular cases where more precision is needed. The current panel of markers for routine profiling will not be readily abandoned because that would necessitate re-analysing all samples in the NDNAD. However, additions to the SGM+ marker set may be driven by harmonisation of marker sets across Europe and the introduction into service of 'mini-STRs' that give more reliable results with badly degraded DNA.

2.23 Eventually STR markers might be superseded by a different type of marker, single nucleotide polymorphisms (SNPs). Technology now exists for typing thousands of SNPs from a biological sample in a single automated operation and SNP analysis is widely predicted to have an important medical role in predicting disease susceptibility, aiding accurate diagnosis, and drug therapy. Such analyses may, in the future, enable more accurate prediction of hair colour, eye colour, ethnicity, etc. from crime scene samples. Furthermore, SNPs would be better than the current SGM+ markers for analysing degraded DNA. Currently such analyses require more DNA than would be yielded by many crime scene stains. In any event, a recent study suggests that SNPs will not replace STRs in national DNA databases in the foreseeable future.[16]

2.24 Experts generally argue that the most promising way of increasing the number of crimes solved by DNA profiling is to focus on obtaining DNA from more crime scenes, rather than modifying current laboratory methods. Trials of mobile DNA analysis laboratories (a Forensic Response Vehicle or 'FRV') have demonstrated the feasibility of obtaining profiles at a crime scene, which could speed up investigations. This might raise issues of the security of the NDNAD, because such a development might require the Database to be remotely accessible using wireless technology which may be easier for non-authorised persons to access.

The interpretation of DNA

2.25 Having described the technical basis of forensic DNA profiling, we note that there still remain issues that a court might raise when presented with DNA evidence. With the original DNA 'fingerprinting' method, there was room for debate over a DNA 'match'. Complete SGM+ profiles are much less ambiguous, although certain features may still require interpretation. Stutter bands – small extra peaks on the graph that are an artefact of the laboratory PCR process – are well recognised and should not normally pose a problem. However, real problems remain with the interpretation of evidence from mixed samples and partial profiles, as detailed below. In addition, a mobile object, such as a cigarette butt, may have originally been dropped somewhere other than where it was found. A forensically sophisticated criminal or a corrupt investigator might deliberately contaminate the crime scene with an innocent person's DNA.

Mixed samples

2.26 Mixed samples are samples that contain DNA from more than one person. Such samples always require interpretation, and a court will need to be satisfied of the validity of the analysis (see Box 2.2). Where two people's DNA is mixed in a 3:1 or greater ratio, the differing peak sizes allow the individual profiles to be disentangled fairly unambiguously (although identification of a very minor component may be uncertain). Interpretation of more equal mixtures depends heavily on the expert opinion of the reporting officer. Profiles provided by known innocent bystanders can be subtracted from the mixed profile to identify peaks of unknown origin. In rape cases, special techniques[17] may identify a male-specific profile from a vaginal swab.

16. Gill P, Werrett DJ, Budowle B and Guerrieri R (2004) An assessment of whether SNPs will replace STRs in national DNA databases *Science and Justice* **44**: 51–5.

17. For example 'laser capture microdissection' or 'Y-specific amplification'.

Partial profiles

2.27 The interpretation of partial profiles or degraded biological samples are of concern. These are profiles that show fewer than the standard 20 peaks of a full SGM+ profile. Sometimes this is because the two marker alleles inherited by an individual from each parent happen to be of identical length.[18] This should be readily apparent from the doubled height of the peak in the profile. Often, however, the cause is a failure of the PCR reaction in the laboratory to work with every allele of every STR ('allele drop-out'). Because there are fewer alleles on which to base a match, the match probabilities are less decisive than for a full profile. Partial profiles require much more skill in interpretation and should always be examined in detail by both DNA experts and ultimately a court.

Contamination

2.28 Contamination, whether deliberate or accidental is another major issue, especially with very small samples. Samples can easily be contaminated with DNA from one of the police or laboratory team if strict preventive measures are not taken. Elimination databases are maintained for the police, for those technicians that visit crime scenes, and those who visit forensic laboratories or who may be involved in the manufacture of items used in the DNA analysis process. These hold the profiles of potential 'innocent donors' of DNA, and hence enable their DNA profiles to be excluded from the investigation. The Police Elimination Database (PED) covers the police and Scenes of Crimes Officers (SOCOs), and the Manufacturers Elimination Database (MED) has the profiles of those who produce the equipment used in DNA analysis, as it was found that DNA profiles were being produced of the people who had been involved in the manufacture of the swabbing kits. Each private company also has databases of its staff.

2.29 These elimination databases ideally contain the profiles of all the people who might contaminate a sample. In theory this should allow such contamination to be identified and the contaminating profile to be 'subtracted' from the crime scene profile. However, many individuals are involved in the transfer of DNA from a crime scene through the process of collection, storage, transport and laboratory analysis. There is also the possibility of transfer of DNA from one crime scene sample to another, or indeed from the biological samples from the crime scene to clothing or other material taken from a suspect. Potential contamination can only be avoided by meticulous control of every aspect of sample collection and processing. It also requires adherence to strict custody controls of exhibits, so that crime scene exhibits cannot come into contact with a suspect at any point.

Very small samples

2.30 While DNA technology has advanced to be able to analyse smaller and smaller samples (see Box 2.2), very small samples present most of the problems mentioned above in acute form. Both allele drop-out and allele drop-in (extra artefactual peaks) can occur, and the risk of contamination is high. Computer programs for identifying individual profiles in mixed samples may be ineffective with very small samples. Selective reporting is also an issue, as laboratories may repeat the PCR reaction several times, and only report those peaks that are seen in at least two replicate runs. There are issues about how such analyses should be reported in court (see Chapter 5).

2.31 However far the science may develop in the future, its current uses are largely restricted to indicating the presence of a person's biological traces at one or several locations at a crime scene. Any determination of other relevant factors, such as how the biological material came to be left there, the time and duration of the person's presence, or the sequence of actions that took place, will need to draw on other kinds of evidence to be taken into account by investigators, advocates, judges and triers of fact (see paragraphs 5.23–5.26).

18. The person is 'homozygous' for that allele.

Conclusion

2.32 Generally speaking, the science and technology of DNA profiling is increasingly robust and reliable. However, there are several continuing risks, especially when the science and the technologies are pushed to their limits. In particular there are dangers of deliberate or accidental contamination, misinterpretation of mixed samples, and mistaken interpretation of partial profiles (and the potential for the misuse of statistics, which we consider in Chapter 5) in establishing the probability of a match. Our recommendations in the following chapters are designed to reduce the risks of mistaken identification and wrongful conviction resulting from (relatively rare) cases of flawed interpretations of the information provided by DNA profiles.

Chapter 3

Ethical values and human rights

Ethical values and human rights

Introduction

3.1 The protection of the public from criminal activities is a primary obligation of the state. However, this obligation must be exercised with due respect for a number of fundamental ethical values and in the light of modern legislation on human rights. Our justifications for adopting one approach to forensic databases rather than another are framed in terms of these ethical values and the legal rights through which they are expressed in the United Kingdom. In this chapter we briefly introduce some of them.

3.2 The values with which we are primarily concerned are *liberty, autonomy, privacy, informed consent* and *equality* (paragraphs 3.4–3.16). These values are not absolute. There is a strong presumption in liberal democracies in favour of not restricting them, but the presumption can be overcome in appropriately circumscribed contexts for compelling reasons backed by appropriate empirical evidence. In the present context the most important overriding consideration is the public interest in the successful investigation, prosecution and conviction of those who commit crime, an aim that, moreover, seeks to promote the value of liberty for the population as a whole (paragraphs 3.4 and 3.19). The method by which we seek to balance these moral goods depends upon whether we take a *utilitarian*, *rights-based* or *duty-based* approach (see paragraphs 3.20–3.23). We broadly endorse a rights-based approach, which recognises both the fundamental importance to human beings of respect for their individual liberty, autonomy and privacy, and the need, in appropriate circumstances, to restrict these rights either in the general interest or to protect the rights of others. The principle of *proportionality*, which is relevant in both ethical and legal debates, is at the heart of many of the recommendations in this Report (paragraphs 3.27–3.28).

3.3 The legally enforceable human rights that are relevant to our justifications include the right to a *fair trial*, the right to *respect for private and family life*, and the right to *equal treatment*. Any interference with these last two rights must be *proportionate* (paragraph 3.32).

Ethical values

Liberty

3.4 In this Report we use the term 'liberty' in two distinct senses. The first is freedom from legal restraint, or what is usually called negative liberty. One could say that liberty in this sense is reduced by police powers to take and retain fingerprints and DNA profiles and samples without consent. Noting this infringement does not imply that one necessarily opposes such powers, provided that they are exercised reasonably and proportionately. The second sense in which 'liberty' is used is to describe the necessary conditions for the freedom which we believe people ought to be able to enjoy in modern liberal societies. For example, we might say that in order to promote the liberty of all citizens, each needs to act in ways that protect both them and others from criminal activities, or in such a way as to avoid unfair discrimination. As this second sense of 'liberty' makes clear, however, we do not equate liberty simply with licence: not every constraint on people to act as they might wish is an interference with liberty, and such constraints may indeed promote liberty in the second sense. For example, even the most minimal state is likely to recognise a responsibility to take action to prevent people from killing or robbing one another, and such action to promote the liberty of the wider population will inevitably involve some form of restriction on the freedom of action of the individual. Nevertheless, we do recognise that a justification must be shown for any infringement of the negative liberty of the individual (see paragraph 3.17).

Autonomy

3.5 There is no single accepted definition of 'autonomy', although as Onora O'Neill notes, most are based on some notion of independence and personal responsibility.[1] For Kant, autonomy means the distinctively human capacity for rational thought and action in accordance with the moral law. It is this capacity which underlies the moral imperative to treat individuals as 'ends in themselves': "So act that you use humanity, whether in your own person or in the person of any other, always at the same time as an end, never merely as a means".[2] Moreover, "he is under obligation to acknowledge, in a practical way, the dignity of humanity in every other human being".[3] Hence, according to Kant, human capacity for autonomy and the value we place on it underpin the moral requirement to treat all human beings with dignity. John Stuart Mill, while rarely using the actual term 'autonomy', places great weight on the 'free development of individuality' as being one of the leading essentials of well-being.[4] Frankfurt,[5] on the other hand, puts more emphasis on the idea of self-governance, describing autonomy as the ability to live our lives in the way we 'truly' wish them to be, instead of simply following our first, perhaps more basic, instincts. In all these definitions, it is useful to note the distinction between a human being's *capacity* for autonomy and the political and material conditions which make it possible for individuals to *exercise* their autonomy. This latter could be characterised either as a moral right arising out of the value placed on that capacity or as a duty to treat human beings in a particular way by virtue of their capacity for autonomous behaviour.

Privacy

3.6 It is generally recognised that every one of us has a protected zone of privacy into which neither the state nor other persons should intrude without our permission. This can be seen as derived from a more basic right to autonomy, or as a precondition for the exercise of autonomy, or as an independent moral principle. The precise derivation of privacy does not matter for present purposes, but it does matter that protection of privacy is not an absolute moral principle. A balance between privacy and other ethical considerations has to be found.

3.7 The precise extent of this protected zone is difficult to define. There are two conceptions that are useful for our discussion: spatial privacy and informational privacy. *Spatial privacy* is "a state of non-access to the individual's physical or psychological self".[6] This is invaded by the non-consensual taking of biological samples and fingerprints, and, to a lesser extent, by unwanted surveillance of the individual. Clearly the principle of respect for bodily integrity comes into play, especially in considerations concerning how samples can be obtained. Activities that not only interfere with a person's privacy but also interfere with their actual body are usually thought to require stronger justification than those that merely infringe informational privacy. It is a basic ethical and legal principle that a person has the right to control access to his or her own body and that interventions in the body require explicit consent, or extremely strong justification.

3.8 *Informational privacy* refers to personal information about an individual that is ordinarily "in a state of non-access to others".[7] This encompasses all the kinds of information about ourselves (which are not already public knowledge) that we would reasonably regard as intimate or

1. See, for example, the discussion in O'Neill O (2002) *Autonomy and Trust in Bioethics* (Cambridge: Cambridge University Press), p28ff).
2. Gregor M (Translator and Editor) (1997) *Kant: Groundwork of the Metaphysics of Morals*, (Cambridge: Cambridge University Press), p38.
3. Gregor M (Translator and Editor) (1996) *Kant: The Metaphysics of Morals* (Cambridge: Cambridge University Press), p209 [first published 1797].
4. O'Neill O (2002) *Autonomy and Trust in Bioethics* (Cambridge: Cambridge University Press), p30.
5. Frankfurt H (1971) Freedom of the will and the concept of a person Journal of Philosophy **68**: 5–20, reprinted in Christman J (Editor) (1989) *The Inner Citadel: Essays on individual autonomy*, pp63–90 (Oxford University Press).
6. Laurie G (2002) *Genetic Privacy: A Challenge to Medico-Legal Norms* (Cambridge: Cambridge University Press), p6.
7. *Ibid.*

sensitive, and which we would therefore want to withhold or whose collection, use and circulation we would wish to control.[8] Some of the information in a person's genome falls within this category, for example information about risk factors for disease or family relationships, but it is disputed whether all genetic information merits strong protection. Where genetic information cannot be linked to a particular, identifiable individual, for example by being anonymised, then there is far less reason to object to its use for research. Similarly, a genetic profile does not in itself disclose sensitive medical information or reveal family relationships, but the related sample linked to an identifiable individual does have such potential. Accordingly, our privacy interests are less strong for a DNA profile compared with a biological sample, and our claims in respect of each likewise differ.

3.9 One aspect of privacy is *anonymity*: "the right of the individual to escape from the intense surveillance situations of small communities".[9] Anonymity gives individuals and families the opportunity to live down their past and to enter into new relationships. Those who have previously engaged in criminal activity may need this to become rehabilitated and to live a decent life. The indefinite retention of biological samples deprives those included on the National DNA Database (NDNAD) of some aspects of this freedom because a match between their genetic material found at any crime scene – and independent of their involvement in the offence – will result in their inclusion in a criminal investigation. Accordingly, there must be sound justification for depriving them of their anonymity.

3.10 'Genetic exceptionalism'[10] suggests that genetic information is qualitatively different from other personal information. This notion may be significant in other contexts, but it is largely irrelevant for our purpose, where what is important is simply that some genetic information is intimate and sensitive, and that the use of that kind of information should be justified.

Informed consent

3.11 In contrast to criminal justice samples taken from those arrested for involvement in a crime, elimination samples taken from witnesses or other volunteers may only be processed in accordance with the consent of the person concerned. The informed consent of individuals, of mature age and full mental capacity, removes any ethical objection based on liberty or autonomy to the taking, processing and retention of biological samples for DNA analysis and of fingerprints. Informed consent in this context operates as a form of legitimisation:[11] the individual may act freely and autonomously so as to give up their right to privacy to a specified extent. There is an important underlying element of trust in such an action, as the police and others with access to the genetic information or fingerprints are, in return, under a duty to respect the terms on which informed consent was given. As Onora O'Neill has said:

> "First, it is important that data are obtained only by acceptable procedures, and in particular that there is no unacceptable coercion or deception… Second, it is important that data are held and disclosed in ways that prevent their use for purposes that lie outside the consent given, or outside the proper procedures of the relevant public authorities."[12]

3.12 Issues arise as a result of the irrevocability of any consent given: if consent to the taking and retaining of samples is to be regarded as a free decision to surrender a certain degree of privacy,

8. Wacks R (1994) *Personal Information: Privacy and the Law* (Oxford University Press), p26.
9. Wood DM (Editor) (2006) *A Report on the Surveillance Society for the Information Commissioner by the Surveillance Studies Network*, paragraph 11.2.1.
10. See the discussion by Manson NC and O'Neill O (2007) *Rethinking Informed Consent in Bioethics* (Cambridge: Cambridge University Press), pp133–45.
11. Beyleveld D and Brownsword R (2007) *Consent in the Law* (Oxford: Hart Publishing), Chapter 11.
12. O'Neill O (2002) *Autonomy and Trust in Bioethics* (Cambridge: Cambridge University Press), p107; and more generally, Manson NC and O'Neill O (2007) *Rethinking Informed Consent in Bioethics* (Cambridge: Cambridge University Press).

the justification for that invasion of privacy will be lost if the consent is withdrawn. We discuss this issue further in Chapter 4.

3.13 Additional issues arise if identifiable samples or profiles on a forensic database are used for research outside the narrow context of identification and police investigations. Normally any kind of research involving identifiable genetic information requires explicit informed consent from the persons from whom the genetic material or information has been derived.[13] The current presumption that consent is necessary in the (genetic) research context is the result of a long historical development where consent requirements have come to be seen as extremely important and one of the ways in which protection of personal interests in autonomy, privacy and bodily integrity can be secured. Although there is an ongoing debate about consent in research and the circumstances in which the consent requirement can be waived,[14] the burden of proof clearly falls on anyone who suggests that a particular kind of genetic research can take place without explicit consent. In Chapter 6 we contend that for non-operational research (that is research that is not directly related to a specific police investigation) using either DNA profiles or the biological sample, there must be safeguards in place that will ensure the irreversible anonymity of the samples. Non-operational research without consent on identifiable forensic samples cannot be justified.

Equality

3.14 The possibility of intensified surveillance of those individuals whose profiles are retained on forensic databases, as potential suspects, leads to the possibility of increased social exclusion of certain groups, such as young males and black ethnic minorities, who are disproportionately represented on the NDNAD (see paragraphs 4.63–4.66). An important issue to be considered is whether this disproportionality is a reflection of police arrest, charge and cautioning processes, or other social or institutional factors, or whether it is a result of an inherent bias in the NDNAD. Police powers to take and retain biological samples and the resulting DNA profiles may aggravate social tensions by discriminating against those who live in police 'hot-spots' or belong to groups more likely than others to be targeted by police.

3.15 The principles usually called upon to help us resolve these issues are those of equality and non-discrimination. While it is difficult to identify a single meaning of these concepts that will be applicable in all circumstances,[15] one meaning, based on the moral premise that people's lives and fundamental interests are of equal worth, is that 'likes' should be treated alike unless there is justification for not doing so. This is regarded not only as a key ethical value, but also as a fundamental principle of justice,[16] and of good administration. It requires "that where the exercise of governmental power results in unequal treatment it should be properly justified, according to consistently applied, persuasive or acceptable criteria".[17] One difficulty is determining who are similarly situated 'likes'. Almost all processes in the criminal justice system involve drawing distinctions between people: those who are victims or witnesses and those who are suspects; those who are suspects and those who are charged; those who are charged and those who are convicted; those convicted of minor offences, and those of serious offences; and between those who are adults and those who are juveniles or children. Although all these distinctions are normally legitimate for the prevention and investigation of crime, other distinctions, notably those based on grounds of race, gender, sexual orientation, religion, age or

13. Human Tissue Act 2004, Part 1.

14. Manson NC and O'Neill O (2007) *Rethinking Informed Consent in Bioethics* (Cambridge: Cambridge University Press).

15. McCrudden C (2002) Equality and Non-Discrimination, in *English Public Law*, Feldman D (Editor) (Oxford: Oxford University Press), p582.

16. See, for example, Lord Hoffmann in *Arthur J.S. Hall v Simons* [2000] 3 All ER 673 at 689.

17. McCrudden C (2002) Equality and Non-Discrimination, in *English Public Law*, Feldman D (Editor) (Oxford: Oxford University Press), p614.

disability, require strict scrutiny if and when they are used as the basis for differential treatment, so as to ensure that they are both appropriate and necessary to achieve a legitimate purpose.[18] This is heavily dependent on the context. For example, the inferring of ethnic appearance (if reliable, see Chapter 6) or evidence of gender from a DNA profile may be argued to be both appropriate and necessary in the search for a suspect.

3.16 A second meaning of equality is that social goods should in principle be distributed among everyone without distinction unless differences can be justified. Accordingly, the state should respect and protect the right of everyone to have an equal opportunity to partake in the 'goods' of social collaboration and no one should have more than an equal risk of suffering any 'evils' that arise through particular social arrangements. Deviations from this principle must be justified. In the context of forensic databases, any unequal distribution across social groups in the likelihood of having a sample taken or a profile entered into the NDNAD must be carefully scrutinised so as to make sure that an unequal burden is not being unjustifiably laid on some specific social group. Overrepresentation of a specific group on the NDNAD compared with other groups, whether defined by class, race, gender, age or some other characteristic, thus demands examination and needs a convincing justification. Indeed, public authorities are now legally obliged to ensure that they take active steps to promote equality in a range of areas, including race, disability and gender.[19] As a result, the Association of Chief Police Officers (ACPO) has recently commissioned an Equality Impact Assessment of DNA profiling, which should lead not only to an explanation of disparities in arrests and inclusions on the NDNAD, but also to active steps to remove any practices that unjustifiably cause those disparities (see paragraph 4.64).

Justifications of invasions of liberty, autonomy and privacy

3.17 The ethical values we have been discussing are important when considering any restrictions that should be put on the ways in which biological samples and fingerprints are obtained, and whether, and for how long, they should be retained. They point towards a default ethical position of requiring consent to the taking and retaining of samples, on the basis that such consent legitimises what would otherwise be interference with an individual's negative liberty and autonomy (see paragraphs 3.11–3.12). Deviations from this default position can be justified in various ways, most notably by invoking the public interest in general. By calling this a 'public interest', we want to emphasise that this is not just an interest of 'the state'.[20] Alternatively, one may invoke a more specific interest in the efficient investigation of crime, or one may claim that someone who has committed a crime has forfeited the full extent of their rights to protection of liberty, autonomy and privacy.

3.18 It is clear that a well-functioning forensic database has the potential to promote the public interest to a significant degree, but to argue convincingly that this justifies overriding identifiable personal interests or rights requires a number of further steps. The different ways in which a forensic database can be managed means that we need to answer specific questions. Which of the different possible arrangements best balances public and private interests? Does retention of profiles or fingerprints until death, for instance, promote the public interest significantly more than, say, retention for 20 years, until the age of 50 or until ten years after last conviction? Conversely, are an individual's interests infringed to significantly different degrees, depending on the time-span? Alternatively, would the public interest be sufficient to justify a database covering *all* citizens, thus avoiding any concerns as to discrimination? (See paragraphs 4.73–4.78.) Like all other areas of

18. In the legal context, legislation prevents status harm from discrimination on particular grounds such as race, gender, sexuality, disability and age.

19. On the duty of the police in relation to racial equality, see paragraph 4.60.

20. For our purposes, it is not necessary to discuss whether this interest is in the final analysis reducible into individual interests or whether there is an irreducible element of a group or societal interest.

policy, it is important that the public interest that is adduced is not merely a hypothetical interest, but that there is convincing evidence that any specific expansion of the forensic Database will actually lead to a significant improvement in the prevention or investigation of criminal acts.

3.19 In modern liberal democracies there tends to be an emphasis on the need to achieve a careful balance between personal liberty and the common good.[21] The greater the threat to social order, the stronger are the arguments for the curtailment of personal freedom. This approach has been very prominent in political discourse in the United Kingdom over a range of issues concerning civil liberties, including the control of serious and organised crime and of terrorism. It is reflected in the case presented to us as part of our consultation by ACPO, the Home Office, the NDNAD, and the Scottish DNA Database and many others, that the relatively small loss of personal liberty involved in taking and retaining DNA samples and profiles is outweighed by the large gains in personal security and social order through the more effective detection and conviction of offenders. At the same time, critics of the increasing use of DNA profiling and the associated Database are concerned that the scientific and technical advances should be compatible with the 'due process' considerations that are of central concern in modern criminal justice systems, with appropriate emphasis on the value of protecting individual privacy, autonomy and liberty.

3.20 The method by which one seeks to resolve these conflicting interests depends on the philosophical approach adopted. Three major approaches are *utilitarian*, *rights-based* and *duty-based*. *Utilitarianism*, in its essential form, holds that there is just one moral principle: to seek the greatest benefit of the greatest number. It is thus one form of consequentialism, where the morality of any action is judged solely in terms of its consequences. A 'pure' utilitarian, therefore, would support increased DNA profiling and sampling if this could be shown to maximise aggregate social welfare. However, those who subscribe to a utilitarianism of the kind espoused by John Stuart Mill believe that 'the free development of individuality' is an essential element of human well-being, and that hence "there is a limit to the legitimate interference of collective opinion with individual independence".[22] They would therefore argue that a key factor in protecting the common good would be a strong emphasis on individual liberty. Thus, although a utilitarian approach does not explicitly include a 'balancing' of competing interests, the very attempt to maximise social welfare would in itself incorporate a balancing exercise.

3.21 The starting point of a *rights-based* theory is different. This holds that certain personal rights, for example the right to life, are so important that they should not be sacrificed for the greater good, nor be subject to coercive interference. Other rights are held to be still important, but subject to qualifications to permit them to be 'balanced' against competing rights held by others. The ethical values highlighted earlier in this chapter such as liberty, privacy and autonomy can readily be framed in the language of personal rights. However, rights-theorists do not always agree on the nature and scope of these rights, nor on the persons who are entitled to them, nor on how apparently conflicting rights should be balanced. An inevitable corollary of a rights-based approach is that, for a right to be meaningful, it must include a duty on another party to respect that right.[23]

3.22 A *duty-based* approach,[24] on the other hand, holds that we are subject to certain moral obligations irrespective of the rights of others, and irrespective of the consequences of our

21. Etzioni A (2006) A communitarian approach: a viewpoint on the study of the legal, ethical and policy considerations raised by DNA tests and databases *Journal of Law, Medicine and Ethics* **34**: 214–21.

22. Collini S (Editor) (1989) J. S. Mill: *'On Liberty' and Other Writings* (Cambridge: Cambridge University Press).

23. For example, person A's right to respect for their privacy is only meaningful if persons B and C have a duty not to invade that privacy.

24. For an account of the advantages of an approach grounded in human obligations or duties, see O'Neill O (2002) *Autonomy and Trust in Bioethics* (Cambridge: Cambridge University Press), pp78–82; see also Brownsword R (2007) Informed consent: to whom it may concern *Jahrbuch für Recht und Ethik* **15**: 1, for a discussion of one variant of this approach, which he calls 'dignitarian'.

actions. One example would be Kant's absolute prohibition on using other human beings merely as a means to an end, regardless of any benefits that might be obtained. One variant of a duty-based theory is a *dignitarian* approach, in which it might be argued that certain actions compromise human dignity, and hence are not permitted, regardless of whether they cause harm to an identifiable individual and regardless of the possible good that might eventuate. Such an approach could, for example, be used when considering issues such as familial searching of DNA databases and the possible use of biological samples for medical and research purposes for which no explicit consent has been obtained: the unauthorised use of such sensitive personal information might be seen as undermining the inherent dignity of human beings, regardless of whether the individual concerned is ultimately aware of what is being done.

3.23 Utilitarian and rights-based theories clearly have quite different philosophical foundations. However, a utilitarian approach of the type put forward by Mill could potentially lead to the same outcome as a rights-based approach that privileged individual autonomy and liberty but recognised that these rights had to be subject to qualification in order to allow for competing rights (for example to protection from criminal activity) to be accommodated. The two approaches recognise, albeit for different reasons, the value to individuals of their personal liberty and their ability to exercise their autonomy, and hence recognise the need for appropriate justification for any interference in the enjoyment of these interests. The main alternative to this kind of liberalism could be said to come from the kind of duty-based approach outlined in paragraph 3.22 above which would not permit any potential benefits to be set in the balance against the fundamental value of human dignity. We believe that the most appropriate approach to the issues considered in this Report is one based on rights, while recognising that the key moral rights identified (to respect for individual liberty, privacy and autonomy) must all be subject to qualifications, to protect both the general interest and the individual rights of others.

The 'no reason to fear if you are innocent' argument

3.24 In the public debate about forensic databases the argument is sometimes put forward that those who are innocent have nothing to fear from being on the NDNAD. This argument ignores any intrinsic value that might be placed on liberty, privacy and autonomy, and focuses solely on the more concrete forms of harm that might come to individuals as a result of inclusion on the NDNAD. Setting aside these broader concerns, however, we consider that the argument is fallacious on its own terms, even if we assume that the justice system is perfect and that no one who is innocent of a crime is ever convicted (an idealisation that has historically never been achieved). There are two principal reasons why the argument is fallacious. First, if innocent, simply being the subject of a criminal investigation by the police can cause harm, distress and stigma. For example, if a person is one of a number of persons investigated in connection with a rape because his DNA profile matches a partial profile of the perpetrator, he may well be harmed by the taint of suspicion, both personally and socially, even if he is never arrested or charged. These problems could be ameliorated if the police always behaved with the utmost sensitivity towards those they investigate, but as long as we cannot rely on that always being the case, harm may well eventuate.

3.25 Second, there are reasons to believe that erroneous implications concerning 'criminality' may be drawn from the mere fact that a person's profile is on the NDNAD, even if inclusion signifies only that they have once been arrested. Indeed, the explicit justification for the extent of the Database is precisely that it is intended to represent the actual or likely criminal community (see paragraphs 4.73–4.77). There is thus little doubt that it is not irrational for a person to object to the retention of their biological sample and DNA profile on the Database if they have never committed a criminal act in their whole life nor will ever do so.

3.26 More substantively, however, the 'nothing to fear if you are innocent' argument cannot, alone, be a sufficient justification for the full extent of police powers. As outlined in paragraph 3.24, we suggest that one's starting point should be the presumption of liberty, which is necessarily accompanied by the importance of keeping governmental and police power appropriately delimited and within the rule of law. Given this starting point, then the government always needs to show a strong reason, backed by objective evidence, that there is adequate justification for interfering with the lives of its citizens.

Proportionality

3.27 The resolution of the antagonistic claims of public interests in crime control and individual interests can be approached through the principle of proportionality. This is a method of analysis in which the ends, means and effects of a particular policy are subjected to a detailed assessment, based on sound evidence. This kind of analysis has the advantages of being rational, coherent and transparent. There are three main formulations of the proportionality principle. The first balancing test requires a *balancing* between the *end* that a law or policy aims to achieve against the *means* used to achieve that end, including the impact on affected persons. Clearly some aims are more important than others, for example to combat serious crime as distinct from minor offences, and are given more weight; and some means are less acceptable than others, for example a law or policy which risks intruding on human rights. A second *necessity* test posits that if a particular objective can be achieved by more than one means, the least harmful of those means should be adopted, that is, one that causes minimum harm to the individual or community. A third *suitability* test is sometimes used: this asks whether the means used are appropriate to the accomplishment of a particular aim.

3.28 The outcomes of a proportionality analysis are a matter of judgment, depending on whether one adopts a standard of *strict scrutiny*, or simply seeks to ensure that the decision is a rational one, in the sense that it is supported by credible reasons. For example, a strict scrutiny approach might lead us to conclude that the indefinite retention of biological samples from those who are not convicted of any crime is a disproportionate means of crime control. On a less demanding rationality approach, one might acknowledge that keeping information on those who have been suspects is a credible way of balancing crime control and due process. Ultimately, these questions have to be determined by a detailed examination of the evidence in each situation. The soundness of the evidence available will be a key factor in determining whether a proposed action is, or is not, proportionate to its likely outcome. In reaching our conclusions on issues such as, for example, the extension of police powers to take biological samples or the retention of these samples, we have therefore looked carefully at the available evidence so as to form judgments about whether the means used are proportionate to the legitimate aim of crime control.

Civil liberties and human rights

3.29 Rights such as privacy and equality were not entrenched in law in the United Kingdom until relatively recently. The classical British view, until at least the mid-20th Century, was that personal liberty is protected from arbitrary interference by the supremacy of Parliament and the rule of law. According to this view, despotic government is prevented by the balance between the Executive, Parliament and an independent judiciary that carries out the will of the elected Parliament. The judge-made principles of private law, such as trespass to the person (e.g. taking a body sample without consent), were applied by the courts to the police and public authorities in the same way as they were applied to private individuals. It was thought not to be necessary or desirable either to enumerate certain freedoms in terms of legal or constitutional rights, or to safeguard them from parliamentary encroachment.

3.30 This classical view was increasingly called into question in the second half of the 20th Century, not only because it did not correspond with the more interventionist activities of the welfare state, but also because of growing disquiet about the capacity or will of Parliament to restrain the Executive. The post-war development of many international human rights instruments (ratified by the United Kingdom), including the European Convention on Human Rights (which the UK strongly influenced), stimulated a new rights-consciousness. This led to a growing body of equality and human rights legislation, including the Human Rights Act 1998. Membership of the EU has also resulted in an expanding body of legislation and case law, on subjects such as the protection of personal data, in the framework of police and judicial cooperation between Member States in criminal matters.

3.31 The Human Rights Act 1998 came into operation in 2000 and made most of the rights contained in the European Convention on Human Rights directly enforceable in the United Kingdom. One of the Convention rights that is relevant to the forensic use of bioinformation is the right to a fair trial (Article 6). Article 6(2) states that "everyone charged with a criminal offence shall be presumed innocent until proved guilty in accordance with law". This reflects the common law principle – sometimes referred to as the 'golden thread' – that 'no matter what the charge, or where the trial', the prosecution must prove the guilt of the defendant beyond reasonable doubt.[25] Protection of the innocent from wrongful conviction has the status of a constitutional principle. This means that bioinformation should never be treated as infallible or conclusive; it must be subject to the same rigorous investigation as any other evidence, and if this process leads to reasonable doubt as to the guilt of the defendant, he or she must be acquitted. The 'presumption' of innocence means not only that the state has this burden of proof, but also that there must be no predisposition to find a person guilty simply because of the presence of bioinformation. Mistakes can happen and the process for dealing with bioinformation must be designed to minimise this risk.

3.32 A second Convention right of relevance is the right to respect for private and family life (Article 8). The Act and Convention reflect our earlier comments that rights are rarely absolute, and that a search for a balance of interests is what is important. Article 8 of the Convention provides an example. Article 8(1) states:

> "Everyone has the right to respect for his private and family life, his home and his correspondence."

However, this is qualified by Article 8(2) which provides that:

> "There shall be no interference by a public authority with the exercise of this right except such as is in accordance with the law and is necessary in a democratic society in the interests of national security, public safety or the economic well-being of the country, for the prevention of disorder or crime, for the protection of health or morals, or for the protection of the rights and freedoms of others."

3.33 Since the implementation of the Human Rights Act, a key question to ask of any state policy is whether it engages a human right. This is self-evident in the current context, particularly when a biological sample is required from a suspect. It was stated by the European Court of Human Rights in the case of *Peters v Netherlands*[26] that "compulsory medical intervention, even if it is of minor importance, must be considered an interference with the right to respect for private life".

25. *Woolmington v DPP* [1935] Appeal Cases 462 at 480 per Viscount Sankey.

26. Appln 21132/93, 77-A, DR 75.

3.34 Where a policy does interfere with a qualified right, such as Article 8, it is then necessary to ask whether the interference with the right is proportionate and necessary. Proportionality is about the policy being founded on relevant and not arbitrary considerations (see paragraph 3.27). Necessity implies that there do not exist any alternatives that achieve the same policy goal in a less intrusive manner. Together these concepts raise the question about whether the current extensive scope of measures in the United Kingdom is necessary to achieve the objectives in question. The possibility of different views on what is appropriate and necessary is shown by the differences between parts of the United Kingdom (see paragraphs 1.3–1.5). However, in the case of retaining bioinformation, the House of Lords held that the position in England and Wales, at least up until 2003, did not breach Article 8(1) (see Box 3.1).

Box 3.1: Bioinformation and human rights: the case of S & Marper

In 2001, the Criminal Justice and Police Act removed the requirement to delete police records from those who were once charged but never convicted of a recordable offence. Subsequently, in the case of *S & Marper*[27] the claimants appealed against the decision to retain their fingerprints, biological samples and DNA profiles after they had been cleared of criminal charges. S, aged eleven, had been charged with, but acquitted of, attempted robbery. Mr Marper, 38 years of age and of good character, was arrested for harassment of his partner but the case was discontinued. The House of Lords held by a majority that retention of bioinformation does not breach Article 8 of the European Convention on Human Rights, because there were safeguards in place to protect against the misuse of retained profiles and biological samples and their retention did not have an impact on the private lives of individuals. Law Lord, Baroness Hale (dissenting on this point) said that there was a breach of informational privacy. However, she agreed with the other four Law Lords that, even if there was a breach of Article 8(1) of the Convention, the breach was proportionate and justified in the detection and investigation of crime. Lord Steyn regarded it as "of paramount importance that law enforcement agencies should take full advantage of the available techniques of modern technology and forensic science. Such real evidence has the inestimable value of cogency and objectivity ... Making due allowance for civil liberties, this phenomenon has had beneficial effects."

The House of Lords also ruled that there was no breach of Article 14, which guarantees equal treatment in the enjoyment of all the other rights protected by the European Convention: they held that the difference between those who have, and those who have not, been the object of police suspicion is sufficient grounds for a legitimate reduction in the privacy rights of the former group, at least as far as the retention of biological samples and profiles can be defined as such a reduction. Prior to changes resulting from the Criminal Justice and Police Act 2001 and the Criminal Justice Act 2003, such a distinction had been formulated in terms of a conviction for a recordable offence; however, the 2001 and 2003 Acts have reformulated the distinction so that one-time suspicion is now a sufficient basis to permanently retain bioinformation: the 2001 Act permitted retention once charges had been brought for a recordable offence, while the 2003 Act now permits retention following arrest for a recordable offence, with no further requirement for charges to be brought (see paragraphs 4.9–4.13). The House of Lords judgment relates to the position after the 2001 Act came into force, but before the further amendments to the retention rules in 2003.

The *Marper* case is soon to be considered by the European Court of Human Rights. In another recent case in the same Court, it was explained that: "As regards the retention of the cellular material and the subsequently compiled DNA profile, the Court observes that the former Commission on Human Rights held that fingerprints did not contain any subjective appreciations which might need refuting and concluded that the retention of that material did not constitute an interference with private life.[28] While similar reasoning may also apply to the retention of cellular material and DNA profiles, the Court nevertheless considers that, given the use to which cellular material in particular could conceivably be put in the future, the systematic retention of that material goes beyond the scope of neutral identifying features such as fingerprints, and is sufficiently intrusive to constitute an interference with the right to respect for private life set out in Article 8 § 1 of the Convention."[29]

27. *R (on the application of S) v Chief Constable of South Yorkshire; R (on the application of Marper) v Chief Constable of South Yorkshire* [2003] 1 All ER 148.

28. See *Kinnunen v Finland*, no. 24950/94, Commission decision of 15 May 1996.

29. Decision as to the Admissibility of Application 29514/05, Hendrick Jan Van der Velden against the Netherlands.

Chapter 4

Criminal investigation

Criminal investigation

Introduction

4.1 Since the first use of a fingerprint in a criminal investigation over a century ago, the forensic use of bioinformation has been invaluable in assisting in the detection and prosecution of crime. Many crimes may not have been solved, or successfully prosecuted, by any other means. Developments in science and technology are increasingly harnessed for the benefit of policing, and are used by prosecution authorities domestically and internationally, in investigations ranging from minor thefts to major terrorist attacks. In addition to the identifications made using the fingerprint database, the National DNA Database (NDNAD) Annual Report 2005–2006 states that between May 2001 and March 2006 there were 182,612 matches between crime scene samples and subject profiles, identifying 165,099 separate individuals who may have been associated with a crime scene. In 2005–06 alone, subject samples were matched with 49,247 crime scene samples. Although only a proportion of fingerprint identifications and DNA profile matches will have resulted in successful prosecutions, it cannot be doubted that many criminals have been, and will continue to be, caught and convicted through the use of forensic bioinformation.

4.2 In this chapter, we consider the ways in which bioinformation is collected and retained for use during criminal investigations. We draw attention to some of the criticisms over the means by which the bioinformation databases have grown, drawing particular attention to issues of consent, equal treatment, the position of minors and the administration of justice. It will be necessary to draw some clear distinctions between situations where the use and retention of DNA profiles or fingerprints does not raise serious ethical issues, but the use or retention of biological samples does raise such issues.

The collection of bioinformation

Fingerprinting

4.3 In England and Wales, the 1891 Penal Servitude Act first provided for the measuring, photographing and fingerprinting of convicted prisoners.[1] Those on remand could only be fingerprinted after a warrant permitting their fingerprints to be taken had been issued by a magistrate, and if they were not subsequently convicted of an offence, their fingerprints were to be destroyed.[2] The call for powers to fingerprint suspects before conviction was not responded to until the Criminal Justice Act of 1948. While concerns were expressed about the extension of powers, the act of taking fingerprints itself was deemed 'unobjectionable' with the now common adage 'only the guilty need worry', used in Parliamentary debate. The requirement to destroy fingerprint records if the person was acquitted remained until the Criminal Justice Act 1967 (which also extended fingerprinting to palms). Police were increasingly frustrated, however, by the continuing requirement to gain the authority of a magistrate to take fingerprints, which was not removed until 1984.

4.4 The enactment in England and Wales of the Police and Criminal Evidence Act (PACE) in 1984 finally granted the police power to take fingerprints without consent if there were reasonable grounds for suspecting the involvement of that person in a criminal offence, and fingerprints would tend to prove or disprove his or her involvement or facilitate the ascertainment of his or

1. Regulations for the Measuring and Photography of Criminal Prisoners, SR & O 1896/762. This provision was continued by the Prison Act 1952 ss16 and 54(3).
2. Leigh LH (1985) *Police Powers in England and Wales*, 2nd Edition (London: Butterworths), p228.

her identity.[3] The Criminal Justice Act 2003 extended these powers to allow the taking of fingerprints without consent upon arrest for a recordable offence. Reasonable force can be used to take fingerprints after arrest, charge or conviction. In view of the high proportion of crime committed by young offenders, it was considered important to be able to compulsorily fingerprint suspects regardless of their age. Scottish police forces are also able to take fingerprints without consent on arrest. Moreover, the Police, Public Order and Criminal Justice (Scotland) Act 2006 brought Scotland into line with England and Wales by allowing police officers to take someone's fingerprints, in any place, on suspicion of a criminal offence and in order to verify identity (to facilitate mobile fingerprinting technology – see Box 4.1). It is an offence to refuse in such circumstances, but the police cannot retain such prints once identity has been confirmed.[4]

Box 4.1: Mobile fingerprinting – Project Lantern

Ten police forces have been testing mobile fingerprint readers in 'Project Lantern': Bedfordshire, Essex, Hertfordshire, Lancashire, North Wales, Northamptonshire, West Midlands and West Yorkshire, as well as British Transport Police and the Metropolitan Police. Project Lantern enables confirmation of driver details when police are carrying out a vehicle check, in collaboration with automatic number plate recognition (ANPR). When police in the pilot areas stop motorists and request verification of their identity, they can ask the motorist to volunteer for a fingerprint check to see if their prints are present on the police fingerprint database, IDENT1. If their fingerprints are located on the database then the police are able to confirm the identity of the individual and ascertain whether there are any outstanding warrants for their arrest, or other details, such as whether they are currently subject to a driving ban. The handheld devices take impressions from the two index fingers of the individual, which can then be checked against the fingerprint database (the crime scene database is not searched). These impressions are not stored, and simply assist the officer, by confirming identity, or by suggesting the driver has provided false details. If the motorist refuses to consent then the officer may find reasonable suspicion sufficient to permit the arrest of the individual, resulting in their fingerprints and DNA being taken at a police station.[5]

Mobile fingerprint devices have also been used in support of police operations at railway stations by transport police. In one operation, where individuals had been stopped and found with knives or other illegal items in their possession, their fingerprints were checked against the national database in an attempt to verify their identity and check whether there were outstanding police matters for which they were sought.

4.5 Fingerprints are now ordinarily obtained using 'LIVESCAN' consoles. The objectives behind the investment in this technology were primarily to: confirm a detainee's identity prior to release (the Metropolitan police have found since installing LIVESCAN, that four per cent of arrestees were providing false details); establish innocence as quickly as possible; link offences to individuals; and identify people with outstanding warrants for their arrest. Each month, more than 100,000 sets of fingerprints are checked upon arrest, and 80,000 marks found at scenes of crimes are searched against IDENT1 (the fingerprint database), with on average 6,000 identifications made (see paragraphs 4.24–4.27). This automated process has dramatically shortened the time taken to perform identifications and circumvents the need to rely upon an arrestee's honesty in giving details of their identity.

4.6 The collection of fingerprints from suspects without consent appears to be widely accepted. Fingerprint recognition systems are proliferating in civil society, to confirm identity, particularly at international borders, and for financial transactions and access control systems. Recent controversy has surrounded the establishment of fingerprint databases in some schools, where they have been introduced to school libraries and canteens. These databases have spread throughout the United Kingdom and elsewhere. This is now being examined by the Government.[6]

3. Authorisation can only be given for the purposes of identification if the person refuses to identify themselves or the officer has reasonable grounds to suspect that he is not who he claims to be: s61(4a). Consent must be given in writing at the police station or can be oral if given elsewhere (s61(2)).

4. S.82 of the 2006 Act.

5. For further information from the National Policing Improvement Agency on Project Lantern, see http://www.npia.police.uk/en/5971.htm, accessed on: 4 July 2007.

6. Jim Knight MP stated in the House of Commons on 29 January 2007 (Hansard, column 68W) that the Department of Education and Skills was consulting the Office of the Information Commissioner and the British Educational Communications and Technology Agency (Becta) about the use of biometric technologies in schools.

4.7 The limited use of mobile fingerprinting means that at present in the United Kingdom, citizens are not yet regularly fingerprinted at the roadside or elsewhere. This may change if the Home Office proposals of March 2007[7] were introduced. These include extending the power to take fingerprints and biological samples without consent immediately from those arrested for a (currently) non-recordable offence. This would mean that individuals would increasingly be fingerprinted and sampled in locations other than police custody suites, and for more minor offences.

4.8 Alongside the investment in DNA technology, the Government has invested approximately £10 million in IDENT1 since 2000. The increase in attendance of Scenes of Crimes Officers (SOCOs) at crime scenes, one of the central aims of the DNA Expansion Programme, has led to a five per cent increase in fingerprints being yielded from crime scenes (in contrast to a three per cent increase in biological sample yields). However, although fingerprints are more readily located at crime scenes, there is a greater 'attrition' rate, with fewer fingerprint yields resulting in a detection (only ten per cent of crime scenes yielding fingerprints result in a fingerprint detection, compared with 20 per cent for biological samples). These results have led to calls for further investment to improve fingerprint detection rates, which could be more cost-effective than further investment in DNA technology.[8]

Taking biological samples

4.9 When the police first began using 'DNA fingerprinting' (see paragraph 2.9), consent was required before biological samples could be taken. However, it became clear that this novel technique could be used more widely if powers were made available to take biological samples without consent. A succession of Acts of Parliament and amendments has eased restrictions on the police discretionary power to take biological samples. The Police and Criminal Evidence Act (PACE) 1984 specified limited police powers to compel criminal suspects to provide samples, differentiating between 'intimate' and 'non-intimate' samples. An intimate sample, which could be taken only with consent, was defined as a sample of blood, semen or any other tissue, fluid, urine, saliva or pubic hair, or a swab taken from a bodily orifice. However, where consent was refused, juries or courts were entitled to draw from this refusal any inferences they deemed appropriate, and to treat the refusal as supporting other prosecution evidence.

4.10 A non-intimate sample was defined as a sample of hair other than pubic hair, a sample taken from a nail or from under a nail, a swab taken from any part of a person's body other than a bodily orifice, a footprint or a similar impression of any part of the body other than a part of the hand (fingerprints were treated separately). Non-intimate samples could only be taken without consent on the authority of an officer of at least superintendent rank who had reasonable grounds for suspecting the involvement of the individual in a serious arrestable offence (see Box 1.2) and who believed that the sample would tend to confirm or disprove this involvement.

4.11 The Criminal Justice and Public Order Act (1994) (CJPOA) extended police powers in two important ways: first, by enlarging their scope to obtain and retain samples and, secondly, by making specific provisions for the speculative searching of the profiles derived from such samples. In relation to the first, the Act redefined mouth samples as non-intimate and empowered the police to take them without consent; it also permitted non-intimate samples to be taken without consent from individuals arrested in connection with the investigation of any 'recordable offence' (as opposed to a 'serious offence' – see Box 1.2). This provision radically widened the 'pool' of criminal suspects from whom samples could be taken and, as a result, when the NDNAD 'went live' on 10 April 1995 it was quickly populated with a large number of

7. Contained in the consultation document *Modernising Police Powers: Review of the Police and Criminal Evidence Act.*

8. Home Office (2005) *DNA Expansion Programme 2000–2005: Reporting achievement* (Forensic Science and Pathology Unit).

DNA profiles.[9] However, the Act also specified that subject samples and profiles obtained from those suspects who had been sampled upon arrest but were subsequently not convicted of a recordable offence were to be removed from the NDNAD.

4.12 The two most significant pieces of legislation since the CJPOA have been the Criminal Justice & Police Act 2001 (CJPA) and the Criminal Justice Act 2003 (CJA). Each of these has further extended the retention regimes that underlie the growth of the NDNAD. The first permitted the indefinite retention and speculative searching of the samples and profiles of all individuals who had been charged with but not necessarily convicted of a recordable offence. The second Act granted powers to take and retain samples from individuals arrested but not necessarily subsequently charged or convicted in connection with a recordable offence. The retention and use of bioinformation from a category of persons who had been subject to police suspicion but whose guilt has not been determined through any judicial process marks an important shift in the relationship between such individuals and the state.

4.13 This means the one-time suspect who may never have been charged and who has no criminal record can now have their DNA profile permanently loaded onto the NDNAD and their biological sample stored. The number of such individuals is considerable: 300,000 are arrested each year in connection with a recordable offence but not subsequently charged. At the end of November 2005, there were 139,463 profiles on the NDNAD that related to individuals who were not subsequently charged or cautioned (this included 15,116 volunteers). At that time, this represented around 4.5 per cent of the total number of profiles on the NDNAD.[10]

4.14 The case of *Marper* signalled judicial approval of the exercise of police powers to take samples up to, and including, the Criminal Justice and Police Act 2001 (see Box 3.1). The House of Lords decided, in the words of Lord Steyn, that "the taking of fingerprints and [DNA] samples from persons suspected of having committed relevant offences is a reasonable and proportionate response to the scourge of serious crime". The case originated before the Criminal Justice Act 2003 (which changed sampling and retention powers) and the Serious Organised Crime Act 2005 (which changed the police arrest powers – see Box 1.2) came into force. There have not since been any legal challenges to the new powers under the 2003 and 2005 legislation.

4.15 In its submission to our consultation, Liberty (the National Council for Civil Liberties) acknowledged that "there are many legitimate reasons why the police may need to take a suspect's fingerprints or DNA during the course of a criminal investigation. This information could, for example help the police to determine whether a suspect was at a crime scene and/or to confirm a person's identity." However, Liberty also highlighted examples of where unnecessary distress or embarrassment was caused in the way samples were taken.

4.16 In taking samples, it is essential that proper ethical standards are observed. For example, samples should not be taken at a time or place that is likely to cause unnecessary inconvenience or distress to the person concerned; the least intrusive method of taking a sample (e.g. a mouth swab) should be used; and particular sensitivity should be shown to vulnerable people particularly minors and others without the capacity to consent.

4.17 Upon arrest for a recordable offence, it is necessary for the police to be able to establish accurately the identity of the individual and it may be essential for the police to obtain fingerprints or a DNA profile to investigate criminal activity that may have been carried out by the arrested individual. An individual arrested for a recordable offence can expect limits to be placed on their liberty and autonomy while the police conduct these necessary inquiries. **It is our view that the authority to take (for impending use in criminal investigation) fingerprints and**

9. In 1995/6, 39,712 subject profiles and 2,881 crime scene profiles were added to the NDNAD.

10. Andy Burnham MP, Hansard, 20 December 2005, column 2890W.

biological samples without consent from those who are arrested on suspicion of involvement in any recordable offence is proportionate to the aim of detecting and prosecuting crime. At the same time, we note that the distinction between recordable and non-recordable offences is to some extent arbitrary (e.g. failing to give advance notice of a procession is recordable, but obstruction of the highway is not). We recommend that the list of recordable offences for which fingerprints and biological samples can be taken from arrestees should be rationalised so as to exclude all minor, non-imprisonable offences.

4.18 The Home Office proposals released in March 2007 include the possibility of abolishing the criteria of 'recordable offence' and permitting the taking of fingerprints and biological samples from anyone arrested in order to "populate identification databases and remove unnecessary operational constraints on the extent to which police are able to use fingerprints etc. to prevent, detect and investigate crime". This is a very considerable extension of police powers and would again alter the nature of the population whose bioinformation is taken and held by the police. It may lead to legitimate questions over whether the NDNAD could still be accurately described as containing the DNA profiles of the "active criminal population"[11], as it comes to encompass an ever larger proportion of the general population. The taking of bioinformation from individuals arrested for the most minor offences may be disproportionate in its effect on the legitimate privacy interests of such individuals, especially if there is no doubt about their identity. Ongoing oversight processes would be required if such proposals were implemented to ensure that arrests could never be made simply for the purpose of 'speculatively' obtaining bioinformation.

4.19 Although many people (including several Law Lords and some respondents to our consultation) argue that the fact of being lawfully arrested by the police on any occasion is an indicator of likely current and subsequent offending, others argue that arrests have to be properly understood. The assertion in the response from the Home Office to our consultation, that arrested persons 'differ' from non-arrested persons, runs directly counter to the statement of the then Home Office Minister Joan Ryan MP that: "As far as we are aware, there is no definitive data available on whether persons arrested but not proceeded with are more likely to offend than the population at large."[12] The National DNA Annual Report 2005/06 states that there have been 200,300 subject profiles on the NDNAD that were retained under the powers of the Criminal Justice and Police Act 2001, which allowed for retention where a suspect was not subsequently convicted of a recordable offence. From these subject profiles, approximately 6,290 individuals have been linked with crime scene samples from some 14,000 offences. Since the Criminal Justice Act 2003 permitted retention of subject samples from those arrested and not proceeded against, there have been matches of profiles retained on this basis with scenes of over 3,000 offences including 37 murders, 16 attempted murders and 90 rapes.[13]

4.20 These statistics are used to justify the retention of subject samples from those arrested but not convicted. However, these statistics give no indication of the significance of the DNA in the police investigation (did the police already have the suspect whose DNA matched to a crime scene in custody or was the DNA match a lead to an unknown suspect?); whether the 'matches' led to any subsequent arrest or conviction; or if the DNA match was used in the investigation or any court proceedings. Further, these statistics may conflict with those given in recent Parliamentary answers (see paragraphs 4.47–4.50). If there is no further, more detailed evidence that retaining the bioinformation of arrestees will achieve improvements in crime control, the

11. This was the stated aim of the Government when announcing in Parliament its investment in the DNA Expansion Programme in April 2000. It has been repeated in several subsequent government statements, and contained in the DNA Expansion Report 2005. It remains Strategic Objective No. 2 in the National DNA Database Annual Report of 2005–2006.

12. Joan Ryan, House of Commons, Hansard, 8 October 2006, column 491W.

13. National DNA Database (2007) *The National DNA Database Annual Report 2005–2006*, p36; John Reid MP, House of Commons, Hansard, 14 December 2006, column 1315W (figures confirmed by the Home Office).

interference with individuals' liberty cannot be justified.

4.21 The implementation of the March 2007 proposals would require further justification. It is difficult to know how effective this measure will be in improving detection rates. Indeed, it is contentious to suggest that adding subject samples in respect of minor offenders, including those whose arrest results in no further action, will reap significant benefit in terms of subsequent crime detection and prosecution. Those arrestees are likely to include disproportionate numbers of children or youths or individuals from ethnic minorities, so exacerbating the current disproportionate representation of youths and ethnic minorities already on the NDNAD. Justifications based upon a possible 'deterrent effect' – that potential offenders may refrain from offending in light of the knowledge that their DNA profile was on the NDNAD – are very difficult to support and remain hypothetical (see paragraph 4.40).

4.22 This extension of arrest and sampling powers would be far less effective than other measures that could be taken, for example, by retrieving more crime scene samples, and may also be less effective than other changes to policing practice or interventions aimed at social factors impacting upon crime. For example, measures such as a greater focus upon proactive or community policing, or investment in drug treatment centres, could equally result in improved detection rates, or reductions in crime. The Home Office proposals (March 2007) are not backed by sound empirical evidence that their implementation would be a proportionate response to criminal activity (see paragraphs 3.27–3.28).

4.23 An arrest permits lawful detention for particular purposes, and alters the legal rights of the arrestee, changing their status from free to unfree. It is thus rightly subject to restrictions and some oversight: an arrest must be made under lawful authority, and discretion must be reasonably exercised. Yet it is the case that police may arrest in circumstances where it may be open to question whether it was 'necessary' and arrest powers may be exercised in a discriminatory way. In some instances, arrests may be predicated upon scant or erroneous information, or prompted by improper considerations. In such instances, it is difficult to justify taking bioinformation from arrestees without their consent for the purposes of potentially solving other crimes (either previously committed or to be committed in the future). This situation can be clearly distinguished from those where an individual has been arrested and then charged with a recordable offence, because the charging process (with the involvement of a Crown Prosecution lawyer) ensures that there is sufficient evidence of unlawful behaviour to justify the taking of bioinformation without consent. This individual will then be lawfully subject to infringements upon their liberty while the criminal process takes its course (for example, by being placed on bail or being required to respond to a court summons). Additionally, policing priorities and practices may lead to the disproportionate arrest of certain populations, such as children and youths, members of ethnic minorities, or vulnerable populations such as the homeless or mentally ill. In light of these concerns, **it is our view that the authority of the police to take and store both fingerprints and biological samples from all arrestees without their consent, regardless of the reason for the arrest, is disproportionate to the aims of identifying a person and of confirming whether or not a person was at a crime scene. Suspicion of involvement in a minor (at present 'non-recordable') offence does not justify the taking of bioinformation from individuals without their consent. Where fingerprints are taken electronically in order to verify an identity, they should be compared only with stored subject records and destroyed once such a check has been completed.**

Uses of bioinformation in criminal investigation

4.24 Each time a fingerprint, a mark or biological sample from a crime scene or a subject DNA profile is loaded onto a bioinformation database, there is the potential for links to be established in four different ways:

- a new set of fingerprints/DNA subject profile of an arrestee may match a pre-existing latent crime scene fingerprint/DNA profile (suggesting that this individual may have been linked to that crime scene at some time);
- a new crime scene fingerprint/profile may match an already recorded individual fingerprint/profile (suggesting an individual who has previously been arrested or volunteered a fingerprint/sample may have also been linked to this new crime scene at some time);
- there may be a match between a new and previously loaded crime scene fingerprint/profile (suggesting that the same individual – as yet unidentified – has been linked to both crime scenes at some time); or
- there may be a match between a new fingerprint/profile and a stored fingerprint/profile (suggesting, for DNA, that two people have the same profile[14] or that the same individual has been sampled twice, see paragraph 1.22).

In each case, if the database produces a 'match' between a new profile and a pre-existing record, it is reported to the police force. This could come from within its own fingerprint bureau, or from a forensic DNA analysis provider. This 'intelligence' will then be used to inform ongoing investigations, instigate new ones, or supplement existing information about criminal activity.

4.25 It is claimed that the forensic use of DNA in routine criminal investigations has facilitated important changes in policing in general, and has improved rates of detection in particular. Some argue that this technology has not merely enhanced existing police investigations, but has begun to replace "the slow, tedious and expensive traditional investigative methods of police interviews".[15] Whilst this may overstate the case, DNA profiling has provided a powerful resource for 'intelligence-led' policing, which proactively targets individuals to either prevent them from committing criminal acts, or to quickly detain them following their offending. The role of science and technology has been pivotal to the implementation of intelligence-led policing, and since 2000 the adoption by the Association of Chief Police Officers (ACPO) of the National Intelligence Model (NIM) makes science and technology central to successful investigations.[16]

The impact upon crime detection

4.26 In paragraph 1.18 we reported that from February 2006 to January 2007, the average number of fingerprint 'identifications' using IDENT1 was 6,324 per month. These are known as 'scene of crime' identifications and refer to the following searches:

- Finger Mark against Tenprints: marks taken from a scene of crime are checked against the national tenprint record database held on IDENT1;
- Tenprint against Marks: the fingerprints taken from an individual are run against the unidentified marks from scenes of crime (SoC) database for potential matches;
- Palm Mark against Palm Print: palm print marks from a scene of crime are checked against the database of palm prints;
- Tenprint against Tenprint: primarily used to establish if people have provided the correct details of identity;
- Mark to Mark: used when a known identity attributed to a mark is searched to check potential connections to other marks.

14. This would be the case for identical twins.

15. Watson N (1999) The analysis of body fluids, in *Crime Scene to Court: The essentials of forensic science*, White P (Editor) (Cambridge: The Royal Society of Chemistry), p325.

16. The DNA Expansion Programme provided £241 million between April 2000 and March 2005, funding the increased collection of DNA and upgrading of the technology involved.

When one of these searches is performed using IDENT1, the top 15 results meeting the minimum accuracy threshold are shown. These 'matches' are then checked manually by a fingerprint specialist. If a fingerprint specialist can confirm a match from one of the IDENT1 results, the fingerprint specialist will then make what is referred to as an 'identification' (and an identification will be recorded for IDENT1 statistical records). However, this is just a preliminary verification and confirmation requires further checks from senior fingerprint specialists.

4.27 Many of these initial identifications will go on to be verified to the point where they can be used to arrest a suspect or for evidential purposes in court, while some identifications could be with a suspect, a victim or another individual with a legitimate explanation for the presence of their fingerprints at a crime scene. Statistics are not collected centrally to indicate what proportion of initial identifications go on to be of use in an investigation or prosecution. Estimates state that approximately ten per cent of fingerprints found at a crime scene will lead to a successful detection (see Box 4.2).[17]

Box 4.2: Policing terminology

- **'Fingerprint identification':** (see paragraph 4.26) the initial verification by a fingerprint specialist of a match produced by IDENT1 between a fingerprint or palm print with either a crime scene print, or a set of tenprints already present on IDENT1.
- **'DNA match':** this can be a *'crime to subject'* match, i.e. the name of a suspect being provided to the police in respect of a recovered crime scene profile, or a *'crime to crime'* match, where two profiles from different crime scene samples match, suggesting the same perpetrator.
- **'Detection':** before a crime is classed as detected there must have been:

  (1) a crime that has been recorded;

  (2) a suspect identified and made aware that the offence will be detected against them; and

  (3) sufficient evidence to charge the suspect with the crime.

  There are two types of 'detection': sanction and non-sanction. A 'sanction detection' is where a suspect has been charged and has received a caution, penalty or punishment, or had the case taken into consideration by a court. These detections count as an 'offence brought to justice', for which the police have targets set by the Government. A 'non-sanction detection' means that although there was sufficient evidence for charging a suspect, no further action has been taken in respect of that offence. There are a variety of reasons that may lead to no further action being taken in respect of a recorded crime.[18]
- **'DNA detection':** These are detected crimes in which a DNA match report was available. This may include cases where no one was convicted of an offence in connection with a crime (a non-sanction detection) but a DNA match report was still available. Such detections will not be included in the 'offences brought to justice' statistics.

4.28 The utility of the NDNAD has been evidenced by data indicating that the chance of a new crime scene profile matching an existing subject profile on the NDNAD is 52 per cent (it is 68 per cent for the Scottish Database).[19] The detection rate when DNA evidence is available is significantly higher, at 40 per cent, than the overall crime detection rate, which stands at 26 per cent.[20] Detection rates of cases with DNA are improved further for certain crimes, for example in domestic burglary the detection rate rises from 16 per cent to 41 per cent when DNA is recovered from the scene.

4.29 However, government assertions of the significance of DNA in the investigation of serious crimes such as murder, manslaughter and rape are difficult to assess, as statistics for these crimes are not collected "as [these] detections are achieved through integrated criminal investigation and not by forensic science alone".[21] There are additional factors:

17. Home Office (2005) *DNA Expansion Programme 2000–2005: Reporting achievement* (Forensic Science and Pathology Unit).
18. For example, if: the offender dies, is taken ill and is unlikely to recover or is too mentally disturbed; the complainant or an essential witness is dead, or refuses, or is permanently unable, or if a juvenile is not permitted, to give evidence; a crime has been committed by a child under 10; the police or Crown Prosecution Service decide no useful purpose would be served by proceeding.
19. National DNA Database (2007) *The National DNA Database Annual Report 2005–2006*.
20. Home Office (2005) *DNA Expansion Programme 2000-2005: Reporting Achievement* (Forensic Science and Pathology Unit), p16.
21. Hazel Blears MP, House of Commons, Written Answers, 1 March 2006.

- First, the criminal investigation process is a complex one. Figure 4.1 indicates just some of the many reasons why cases fail to proceed through the criminal process to result in a conviction (this is known as 'attrition'). The existence of a DNA match may reduce attrition, but there remain other significant influences on the crime detection rate.
- Second, many crimes do not have an obvious crime scene, and forensic examination is impossible or not required. In addition, as the Home Office states with regard to minor crimes, for example, "in many cases of minor interpersonal violence, DNA is relatively easily recovered but makes no material impact on the subsequent investigation as the identities of those involved are frequently not in question".[22] Fewer than 20 per cent of crime scenes are forensically examined[23] and DNA profiles are successfully added onto the NDNAD from just one in twenty of these examined scenes.
- Third, there is wide variation between police forces in the proportion of crime scenes that are examined and the number of biological samples that are sent for analysis.

4.30 At the inception of DNA testing, the police and forensic providers distinguished between DNA testing for 'intelligence' (that which could direct police inquiries) and that which could constitute 'evidence' (proof that could be used in court against a defendant). Indeed,

Figure 4.1: Attrition within the Criminal Justice Process

Some typical problems impacting upon the number of offences brought to justice. An 'offence brought to justice' is counted as also including cautions, reprimands and fixed penalty notices as well as criminal convictions gained after a guilty plea or a trial.

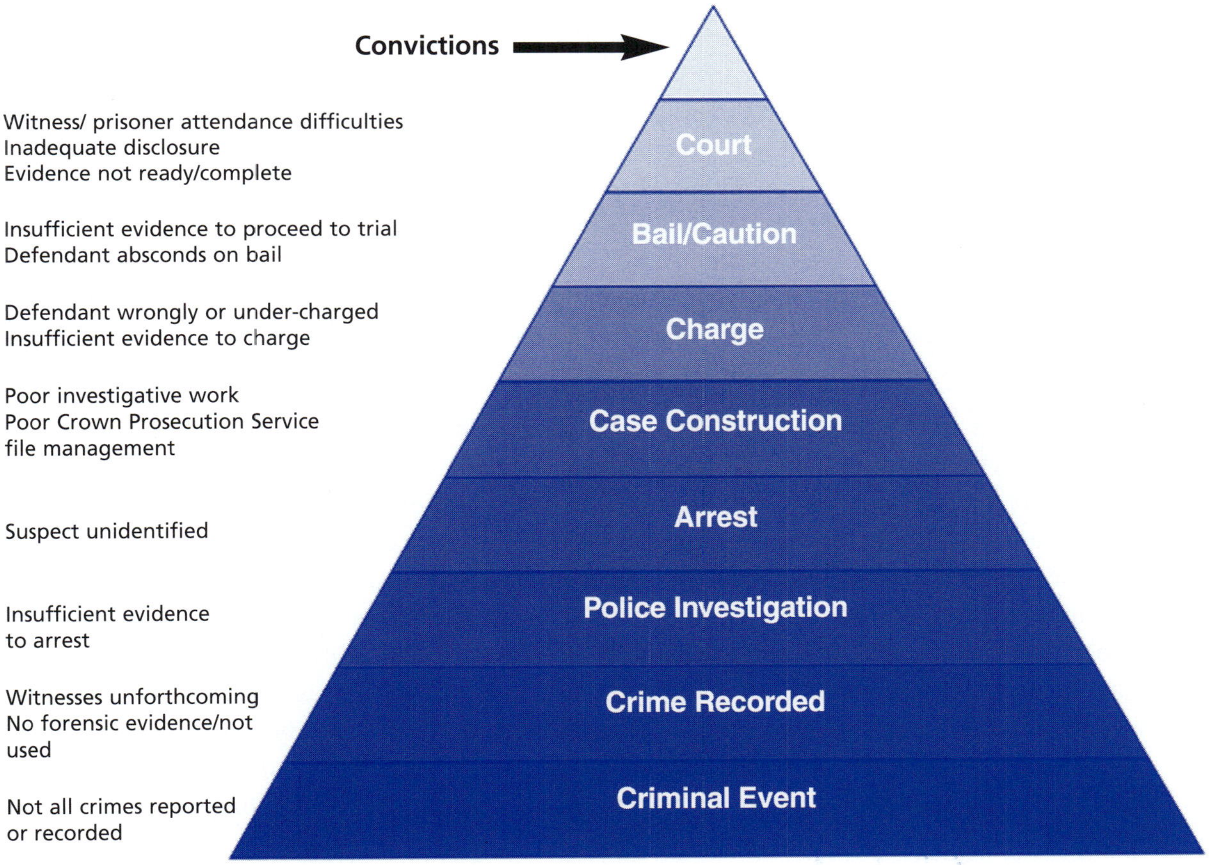

22. Home Office (2005) *DNA Expansion Programme 2000–2005: Reporting achievement* (Forensic Science and Pathology Unit), p16.
23. National DNA Database (2006) *The National DNA Database Annual Report 2003-2004*, p16

throughout official literature, emphasis is put on the use of bioinformation as 'intelligence', that is in providing actionable information that is helpful in giving direction to police investigations. However, with the introduction by the Crown Prosecution Service of the 'staged reporting' process (see paragraphs 5.4–5.5) and the replacement of the original requirement for two DNA sampling tests (one for investigation, then another for 'evidence' if a suspect was charged) with the one 'PACE' sampling kit used for both purposes, it is now clear that a DNA sample can fall into either category. This then supports an argument for *all* DNA use to be subject to the same levels of scrutiny. In our view, the existence of 'intelligence' uses should not lead to a lowering of the highest evidential standards when collecting, processing and using biological materials, even for purposes that may not result immediately in a prosecution. As we discuss in Chapter 3 (see paragraphs 3.24–3.26), there are significant personal costs for citizens who are caught up in police investigations, who may well be entirely innocent, and any police 'intelligence' may later be relied upon in court and scrutinised as evidence.

4.31 The Police Standards Unit has been instrumental in a number of operations aiming to assist victims in unsolved cases; to finalise old or forgotten 'cold' cases; and to use scientific developments to secure more convictions. All 'cold cases' reviewed as part of operations (such as Operation Sapphire, which re-opened 300 unsolved sexual assaults from the 1980s and 1990s, leading to eleven convictions for rape), were selected from unsolved cases with available crime scene samples. Some of these cases were 10 to 15 years old and may have been put to one side because best efforts to solve them at the time had been to no avail. The development of the latest DNA techniques had permitted the 're-invigoration' of these cases.

4.32 Operation Advance, which commenced in 2004, upgraded DNA crime scene samples from unsolved cold cases, in order to attempt to use newer DNA profiling technologies to be able to compare them with profiles on the NDNAD. A sample of 215 crime scene samples were selected, of which 112 were upgraded to SGM+. Of these, one in four subsequently led to a match on the NDNAD, a significant increase. Operation Advance has so far resulted in 22 convictions. A further operation, Advance II, involved very early cases using 'QUAD' which was a DNA profiling technique used in 1994/5. A total of 66 cases were identified as being suitable for further analysis, resulting in 22 matches against the NDNAD, leading to three arrests. In addition to further matches, Operation Advance looks at criminal careers and uses DNA profiles to track offending patterns. The Operation is now starting further work on cases where the evidence consisted of 'DNA mixtures'. 'Familial searching' techniques have also been used to find partial matches in two cases where matches on the NDNAD had been lacking (see paragraphs 6.6–6.11).

4.33 The usefulness of DNA in generally improving poor criminal detection rates, and helping to obtain convictions in previously unsolved cases, has been evidenced partly by the presentation of summary statistics and partly by reference to more anecdotal case studies. However, there is little systematic knowledge of the most effective methods of collecting, recording, processing and using forensic bioinformation. The available information shows a very complex picture. Not all fingerprint and DNA matches lead to a conviction, or even an arrest. Initial DNA match reports are often accompanied by caveats, with 49 per cent of NDNAD matches leading to a crime being detected (see Box 4.2). Moreover, in 42 per cent of cases where DNA evidence was available, the police *already* had the name of the suspect whose identity was suggested by the match report. In 2004–05, the Home Office reported a total of 19,873 'DNA detections' (see Box 4.2), with DNA evidence proving to be of use in a small proportion (0.8%) of all crimes recorded. In many crimes, such as fraud or public order offences, even if DNA were available it would be of little significance.[24] The difficulties in interpreting the value of DNA matches and

24. All figures taken from Home Office (2005) *DNA Expansion Programme 2000–2005: Reporting achievement* (Forensic Science and Pathology Unit), pp12–15.

their support of investigations are magnified by recent Home Office statistical confusion, with conflicting accounts being published and given to Parliament in response to questions about the NDNAD (see paragraphs 4.47–4.52).

4.34 In addition to the initial cost of the DNA profiling of the sample, the private companies that perform the DNA analysis charge approximately £4.50 for the first five years of storage of each biological sample, and slightly under £1.00 for each year thereafter. With the number of samples now standing at four million, this is a considerable drain on police budgets, and costs will increase as the NDNAD expands (not least because of energy costs involved in keeping an increasing number of biological samples frozen).

4.35 **In light of the discussion in this chapter of the usefulness of bioinformation in the investigation of crime, we recommend that:**

- **Expenditure for expert crime scene analysis should be given higher priority than the increased collection of subject samples. If the Government is right to assert that "the whole of the active suspect criminal population is now held on the NDNAD", then further improvements in DNA detection rates rest heavily on expanding crime scene collection rates and ensuring that full use is made of the material collected.**
- **There should be improved recording of police data on the uses of DNA matches and the production of better statistics to inform key stakeholders and the wider public. More effort should also be made to ascertain 'best practice' within policing to maximise the crime control potential of bioinformation. The collation of statistics would also assist with an exploration of the cost-effectiveness of the forensic use of bioinformation and may provide evidence as to whether infringements on the liberty, privacy and autonomy of individuals are justified.**
- **To justify the interference with the liberty and autonomy of citizens, more detailed independent research on the contribution of bioinformation to criminal justice is required.**

Retention of bioinformation

4.36 The retention of bioinformation is highly controversial. Fingerprints and DNA profiles are retained on their respective databases until the individual reaches 100 (or until they die in the case of IDENT1). The retention of fingerprints and DNA profiles raise similar issues, because these are useful only for identification and for matching with crime scene samples (but see paragraphs 2.15–2.21). The permanent retention of fingerprints is not normally considered problematic. However, the functioning of IDENT1 may raise concerns surrounding the 'linkages' with not just the Police National Computer (PNC), but other biometric and informational databases in the future (see Chapter 7). If such linkage were to be permitted (this would require changes in policy and law) then this 'inter-operability' may open up greater possibilities: for wrongful or inappropriate access; for intrusive research; or for misuse. The increased likelihood of identifiability might lead to greater risk of breaches of privacy, and for mistakes during inputting and transferring of data.

4.37 When DNA profiling was introduced, it was argued that the requirement to destroy records from those not convicted limited its potential. Further pressure on the Government to change the law arose from the joint failure of police and the Forensic Science Service (FSS) to ensure the removal of profiles from those who had never been convicted. In 2000, Her Majesty's Inspectorate of Constabulary revealed that more than 50,000 samples and profiles were being held unlawfully, as the law had demanded their removal because the donor had not been subsequently convicted of an offence. Matches between subject profiles that should have been removed and newly entered crime scene profiles proved highly problematic for the courts, with palpably guilty persons appealing against their convictions on the basis of the use at trial of illegally retained evidence.

4.38 In 2001, Parliament removed the requirement to eliminate records, deciding that the retention and indefinite use of samples and profiles taken from those who were once *charged* with a recordable offence, even where they were never convicted, struck an acceptable balance between the interests of the criminal justice system and individual rights. The Criminal Justice Act 2003 extended retention of fingerprints and biological samples to all individuals *arrested* for recordable offences, regardless of whether they were subsequently charged. The Home Office proposals (March 2007), if introduced, would further extend this to all arrestees (regardless of offence), and would entail yet greater permanent retention of bioinformation from individuals who have never been charged with, or convicted of, an offence, and whose innocence must be presumed.

4.39 It is clear that the construction of bioinformation databases to retain large numbers of records and biological samples from individuals is central to efforts to increase crime detection rates (particularly in 'volume' crime). The presence of a DNA 'match' between a suspect and crime scene can dramatically accelerate an investigation and prosecution. Much expense and distress can be spared in reaching a verdict swiftly, particularly if fingerprint or DNA evidence can prompt a guilty plea to be entered by the suspect at an early stage. Bioinformation can also be useful in eliminating from an investigation citizens who falsely confess to crimes or who may come under suspicion but are innocent. The exclusion of innocent suspects from investigations at an earlier stage increases the chance of detecting more quickly the true perpetrator, and also prevents possible wrongful convictions.

4.40 In addition to such benefits, the Home Office also posits that the increased knowledge among offenders that they are likely to be caught may act as a powerful deterrent. Home Office policy relies on the supposition that samples taken for minor offences produce matches with more serious crimes (such examples feature prominently in publicity). Research is also cited that indicates that offenders 'progress' in their criminal careers, stressing that such careers can be 'cut short' by swift intervention of the criminal justice system, facilitated by the use of databases.[25] However, such 'career criminals' (if they were to be found on such databases), must form an increasingly small proportion of people on the NDNAD, with diminishing returns in terms of crimes detected (and careers stymied), relative to numbers of profiles held.

4.41 While the vital importance of greater retrieval and inclusion of crime scene samples is widely recognised, questions remain over the utility of continuing expansion of the NDNAD in terms of capturing individual profiles from ever greater categories of individuals (originally the convicted serious offender, to now, the one-off suspect of a minor offence and consenting volunteers). Whether all of those currently included are 'relevant' for detection purposes has yet to be convincingly evidenced (see paragraph 4.20). If the DNA Database is to assist in the detection of future crimes, why include individuals who are unlikely to offend in the future?

4.42 In any assessment of the retention of bioinformation, there are two critical questions. The first is what are the purposes of bioinformation and its retention on a database? Secondly, is there evidence to support the contention that the retention of samples from those never convicted (or charged) of an offence aids crime detection? In answering the first question, it is only by identifying objectives that we can gauge whether current procedures are justified. A DNA database of profiles is not necessary, for example, if the police wish to confirm whether a biological sample at a crime scene and the DNA of an already arrested suspect match because DNA can be obtained from the suspect and matched (or not) with the crime scene evidence. The database of profiles obtained from crime scene samples becomes useful in attempts to verify whether this person might also be

25. See Leary R and Pease K (2003) DNA and the active criminal population *Crime Prevention and Community Safety* **5(1)**: 7–12; Townsley M, Smith C and Pease K (2005) Using DNA to Catch Offenders Quicker: Serious detections arising from Criminal Justice Samples Jill Dando Institute of Crime Science, available at: http://www-staff.lboro.ac.uk/~ssgf/KP/2005_DNA_to_Catch_Offenders.pdf, accessed on: 5 July 2007.

implicated in a past crime. In addition, the inclusion of this suspect's profile on the NDNAD may provide an easy detection in any *future* crime that they might commit.

4.43 Forensic DNA profiling has been rightly celebrated, particularly in the United States, for its power to exonerate the innocent. Indeed, the matching of DNA profiles with crime scene samples may have saved many innocent people from coming under suspicion, or has ensured the swift termination of inquiries into an innocent suspect, and continues to do so. However, a database is of limited use in re-investigating or overturning wrongful convictions because a clear indication that an innocent individual has been arrested (and hence the risk of a wrongful conviction has been raised) will already be given when the convicted person's DNA profile is shown not to match the relevant crime scene sample. A database is therefore not needed for this purpose. Clearly, the retention of the crime scene profile (especially when it is a partial profile) on the NDNAD after there has been a conviction allows a disputed conviction to be revisited if a *future* subject profile from somebody other than the convicted defendant is found to be a match. Yet present practice is to remove all crime scene profiles once there has been a conviction relating to that crime. This deletion, carried out for administrative convenience, thereby prevents the possibility of any future matches with newly loaded samples from different individuals. This limits the potential for the NDNAD to assist with overturning wrongful convictions.

4.44 The retention of biological samples raises greater ethical concerns than the digitised DNA profiles, as well as practical issues, but at present many jurisdictions retain the biological samples on the same basis as they retain the DNA profiles. The Federal Bureau of Investigation (FBI) in the United States argues that there are compelling reasons to archive biological samples in addition to the digital DNA profiles, and destroying the biological samples would make it impossible to:

- regenerate the database if it were corrupted in some way;
- introduce new, more sophisticated analytical technologies that would require a re-typing of the original sample; and
- perform necessary quality assurance checks including return to re-type the biological sample to confirm the accuracy of existing profiling.[26]

4.45 Other European countries have not found it necessary to have such wide powers of retention as England and Wales. We have already described in paragraph 1.26 how Scotland has taken a different route, allowing indefinite retention only on conviction of an offence, and time-limited retention for people charged with (but not convicted of) sexual or violent offences. In all other cases, samples and information derived from them must be destroyed if the accused or arrestee is not convicted of an offence or otherwise subject to judicial disposal. The arrangements in some other European countries are set out in Box 4.3.

4.46 The United Kingdom Government makes similar claims to those of the FBI for the retention of both the biological sample and DNA profile and adds that:

- it would hinder the administration of justice if samples that should have been destroyed were in fact retained and their use subsequently challenged;
- the withdrawal of consent (of a volunteer) could be a precursor to criminal activity; and
- it is administratively convenient to keep the DNA data.[27]

However, the Human Genetics Commission argued in 2002 that these rationales for retention are not particularly compelling. The Commission, like the Irish Law Commission and the not-for-

26. Herkenham MD (2006) Retention of Offender DNA Samples Necessary to Ensure and Monitor Quality of Forensic DNA Efforts: Appropriate safeguards exist to protect the DNA samples from misuse *Journal of Law, Medicine & Ethics* **34(2)**: 380–4.

27. UK Government (2005) *Forensic Science on Trial: Government Response*, p6.

profit group GeneWatch UK, concluded that other means can be found to assure quality, and that further samples could be re-taken from offenders if necessary.[28]

4.47 The second critical question remains: is there sound evidence to support the supposition that the retention of samples from those never convicted (or charged) with an offence aids crime detection? Serious problems arise when trying to determine the significance of the number of 'matches' with profiles from the unconvicted (see paragraph 4.20).

Box 4.3: Collection and retention in other European countries[29]

The majority of European nations focus on collecting and retaining samples from certain types of serious offender. Many limit the types of offences for which the police can *obtain* non-consensual samples: for example, in Austria police may only collect DNA from certain suspects of 'severe' crimes (such as crimes against the person) and in Finland, Norway, the Netherlands, Hungary and Sweden sampling is limited to crimes that attract specific terms of imprisonment as a punishment (in Finland six months, Norway two years, Sweden two years, the Netherlands four years and Hungary five years). In Belgium, a suspect may be required to provide a biological sample when the crime under investigation attracts a term of imprisonment of five years or more and when biological material relevant to the investigation has been recovered from the crime scene. On the other hand, in the Baltic States of Estonia, Latvia and Lithuania, samples may be taken without consent from all those suspected of involvement in a crime.

Regimes governing the *retention* of profiles of convicted offenders vary greatly. Austria, Estonia and Finland retain such profiles indefinitely, or at least until after the death of the offender, whereas Sweden removes profiles ten years after the end of the sentence; Hungary 20 years after sentence expiry; and France 40 years after sentence or when the individual reaches the age of 80. Profile storage times vary in the Netherlands according to the seriousness of the crime (retention for 20 years if convicted of a crime with a potential sentence of between four and six years and retention of 30 years if convicted of a crime with a potential sentence longer than six years), whereas the Czech Republic requires three-year reviews after conviction. In Belgium, only DNA profiles from those convicted of some violent or sexual crimes can be indefinitely retained. German law requires that a suspect be deemed to be at risk of committing a recordable offence in the future before their profile can be entered on the national database.

Sample retention also varies. In the majority of countries, the fate of samples largely follows that of profiles, although there is not always specific legislative provision which specifies sample retention or destruction. However, in Belgium and Germany, all samples taken from individuals have to be destroyed after successful profiling, and in Switzerland all samples must be destroyed within three months of the entry of the relevant profile on the database. Proposed Italian legislation envisages the destruction of samples following successful profiling. Other than England and Wales, no European jurisdiction systematically retains the profiles or samples of individuals who have not been convicted of a crime, although some states require suspects or prosecuting authorities to request removal once proceedings are ended.

In January 2006, after a detailed report by the Law Reform Commission, the Irish Government proposed the establishment of a national DNA database. The Criminal Justice Bill 2007 is extending police powers to take and retain biological samples from more offenders and also those not convicted, while the Criminal Justice (Forensic Sampling and Evidence) Act 2007 sets out the operation and oversight of the Irish DNA Database. An 'Oversight Committee' will be established at the same time as the Database, which will review and report annually to the relevant minister on the operation of the Act.

4.48 In December 2006, it was reported in Parliament that, since May 2001, 200,000 samples and profiles had been taken from charged but unconvicted individuals (but no figures were given for the arrested but uncharged).[30] The National DNA Database Annual Report 2005–2006 (published in May 2007) details an exercise carried out in November 2005 that showed that the number of individuals on the NDNAD who had not been charged or cautioned at the cessation of inquiries involving them was 139,463 (this figure included 15,116 volunteers).[31] The Home Secretary stated that as at 14 July 2006, 2.3 million persons on the NDNAD had a criminal record (of a total of 3.5 million).[32] Although some of the remaining 1.2 million may be 'replicates', or are awaiting trial, and almost 20,000 were the profiles of volunteers, it is still clear that the

28. Human Genetics Commission (2002) *Inside Information: Balancing interests in the use of personal genetic data* (London: Department of Health); Law Reform Commission (2005) *The Establishment of a DNA Database* (Dublin: Law Reform Commission); GeneWatch UK (2005) *The Police National DNA Database: Balancing crime detection, human rights and privacy* (Buxton: GeneWatch UK).
29. See Williams R and Johnson P (2005) *Forensic DNA Databasing: A European perspective, Interim report*, available at: http://www.dur.ac.uk/sass/casr/projects/?mode=project&id=31, accessed on: 5 July 2007, for a detailed report on the situation in other European nations.
30. John Reid MP, House of Commons, Hansard, 14 December 2006, column 1315W.
31. National DNA Database (2007) *The National DNA Database Annual Report 2005–2006*, p32.
32. John Reid MP, House of Commons, Hansard, 13 December 2006, column 1108W.

number of samples from individuals never convicted of an offence was considerably greater than had previously been reported. This revelation prompted a rash of media headlines, proclaiming that one third of the NDNAD profiles (over one million) were from 'innocent' people (i.e. not charged or not convicted). The Government informed Parliament that the results of a cross-searching exercise performed on the Police National Computer (PNC) on 14 July 2006 showed that at that date, 79.3 per cent of those on the NDNAD who also had an entry on the PNC[33] had a conviction or a caution (i.e. a criminal record). The remaining 20.7 per cent were: persons who had been arrested for a recordable offence where no further action was taken; persons who had been charged with a recordable offence where proceedings are ongoing; and persons under 18 who had a formal warning or reprimand recorded on the PNC.[34]

4.49 The NDNAD Annual Report 2005–2006 states that there are ongoing efforts to establish accurately how many records on the NDNAD relate to 'Criminal Justice arrestees' (individuals who had never been charged with an offence). The accuracy of such data is vital for assessing the benefits of retention of bioinformation from all of those arrested, especially where the benefit has to be weighed against the detriment to civil liberties and risks to privacy. If the number of matches declared as resulting from the profiles of 'innocent' individuals is measured as a proportion of over one million such profiles, this is far weaker support for retention of these profiles than if understood as a proportion of the 139,000 'innocent' profiles, i.e. those who were arrested but no further action was taken, that has also been reported.

4.50 Many respondents to our consultation assumed that the large-scale retention of bioinformation from those who had not been convicted of a recordable offence had had a positive impact upon crime and detection rates, but the reality is more complex. The joint response on behalf of the Association of Police Authorities, ACPO and the Home Office stated that the retention of bioinformation "may well represent a significant time and cost saving in future investigations and help in the prevention and detection of crime". Indeed, the NDNAD Annual Report 2005–2006 reported that:

> "Of the 200,300 or so profiles on the NDNAD that have been retained under the CJPA 2001 and would previously had to have been removed, approximately 8,500 profiles from some 6,290 individuals have been linked with crime scene sample profiles from some 14,000 offences. " (See also paragraph 4.19.)[35]

Matches made to previously unsolved offences would have been possible under the earlier legislation because they do not require the retention of profiles when individuals are not proceeded against or are acquitted.

4.51 GeneWatch, in its response to our consultation, questioned the quality of these and other recent Home Office statistics, suggesting that information about matches is not always supplemented by information about detections, and almost never by information about successful prosecutions. The organisation also points out that "...despite a significant increase in the number of individuals on the database, DNA detections have not increased over the past 3 years", having stabilised at about 20,000 each year. They argue that this is because "many more people now being added to the database are unlikely to commit the type of future crimes for which DNA evidence is relevant." It remains difficult to test this claim, as well as many other more positive claims for the effectiveness of the NDNAD in general terms, without better information than is currently available about the course of investigations and prosecutions where DNA has been recovered from crime scenes.

33. So excluding volunteers, who will not have an entry on the PNC.

34. Joan Ryan MP, House of Commons, Hansard, 19 June 2007, column 1772W.

35. National DNA Database (2007) *The National DNA Database Annual Report 2005–2006*, p36; John Reid MP, House of Commons, Hansard, 14 December 2006, column 1315W (figures confirmed by the Home Office).

4.52 It is clear from the preceding paragraphs that the evidence used in support of the retention regime in England and Wales is seriously limited and confusing. While steps are being taken to try to improve the reporting capabilities of the NDNAD, there is a clear need for more detailed enquiries to be made into the benefits of the NDNAD in actual criminal investigations. In particular, information is needed on how DNA matches may eventually translate (or not) into convictions in different situations, and for different offences. There is very limited evidence indeed that the retention regime of England and Wales is effective in significantly improving detection rates, above and beyond that which may be achieved by retaining only those profiles taken from individuals convicted of a recordable offence (as is the case in Scotland), or by simply searching against stored profiles, but not retaining the DNA profile indefinitely. The match rates between stored subject profiles and new crime scene profiles loaded onto the NDNAD in England and Wales, which is 52 per cent, can be contrasted with that of the Scottish DNA Database, which has a higher match rate of 68 per cent. This demonstrates clearly that the more limited retention policy in Scotland does not necessarily negatively impact upon its subsequent match rates (see paragraph 4.28).

Retention of fingerprints, profiles and samples

4.53 The retention of fingerprints or DNA profiles does not (at this time) permit the police access to more detailed information about an individual. A fingerprint cannot reveal anything about the personal characteristics of an individual, and current DNA profiles are limited, making it difficult for the profile to reveal further, or sensitive, information (see Chapter 2 for details). It is, however, entirely possible to sequence part or all of an individual's entire genome from their biological sample, and therefore, the retention of biological samples requires much greater critical attention, and justification. It is our view that electronic retention of fingerprints and DNA profiles is much less contentious than the retention of biological samples and incurs very little cost. However, there is, at present, a lack of convincing evidence that retention of profiles of those not charged with or convicted of an offence has had a significant impact on detection rates and hence it is difficult to argue that such retention can be justified. **Accordingly we recommend that independent research should be commissioned by the Home Office to assess the impact of retention. In the light of the findings of that research, an informed judgment could then be made.**

4.54 The current practice of indefinitely retaining biological subject samples from those not charged or convicted of an offence is expensive and is the focus of considerable public disquiet and mistrust about possible future uses to which the samples might be put. Our approach is guided by the principle of proportionality (paragraphs 3.27–3.28), bearing in mind the purpose of retaining the bioinformation on the one hand, and the absence of satisfactory empirical evidence to support the present practice in England, Wales and Northern Ireland on the other. **We recommend that the law in England, Wales and Northern Ireland should be brought into line with that in Scotland. Fingerprints, DNA profiles and subject biological samples should be retained indefinitely only for those convicted of a recordable offence. At present, the retention of profiles and samples can be justified as proportionate only for those who have been convicted. In all other cases, samples should be destroyed and the resulting profiles deleted from the NDNAD. This should be reviewed in the light of the findings of the further research that we have recommended.**

4.55 **The Scottish practice of allowing retention of samples and profiles, for three years, from those charged with serious violent or sexual offences, even if there is no conviction, should also be followed. Thereafter the samples and profiles should be destroyed unless a Chief Constable applies to a court for a two-year extension, showing reasonable grounds for the extension.** *(For specific recommendations about the retention of bioinformation from volunteers and minors see below.)*

4.56 It is reported that since 1995, 121,522 crime scene samples and profiles have been removed from the NDNAD, including 30,589 in 2005/06 alone. These are removed after a conviction has been secured in relation to that offence and a decision has been made that it will no longer be investigated. However, this practice is being re-considered by the NDNAD Strategy Board. Permanent retention of crime scene samples would permit not only the possible identification of further potential suspects who may have been involved in an offence, but also allow for the possibility of rectifying possible miscarriages of justice in the future. The fallibility of the criminal justice process, and forensic science, remains clearly demonstrated by cases such as that of Damilola Taylor.[36] **We therefore recommend that, because crime scene samples are unique and unrepeatable, they must be retained indefinitely.**

Victims and volunteers

4.57 Individuals may be asked by the police to volunteer biological samples as part of a criminal investigation. Until 2001, biological samples voluntarily provided to the police could only be used for one-off comparisons against crime scene samples. If these failed to produce a match, samples and profiles were destroyed following the conclusion of an investigation. The inability of the police to retain samples given by volunteers gained media attention after an intelligence-led screen during the investigation of the murder of Louise Smith in 1996. That investigation saw the screening of over 4,500 volunteers. The screen failed to produce a suspect (although a local man was subsequently convicted) but 9,000 local people, led by Smith's parents, signed a petition requesting that the police retain the samples collected during this and future mass screens. In 1999, the Home Office recommended a 'separate voluntary database' which would not be continuously speculatively searched but could be used for elimination purposes. However, subsequent legislation simply allowed for the permanent inclusion on the NDNAD of voluntarily obtained samples.

4.58 Individuals requested by the police to volunteer samples – for elimination purposes, or during a mass screen – may consent to the use of their bioinformation in relation to the investigation of a specific offence, after the conclusion of which the fingerprint, profile and sample are all destroyed. Alternatively, they may now also consent to the permanent retention of their bioinformation. This latter consent is described (at least in the form provided to the individual) as irrevocable. Guidance to officers for taking volunteer samples is contained in PACE Codes of Practice, Code D. This states that the person should be informed of the reason for taking the sample, if appropriate the grounds on which the relevant authority to take the sample has been given, and that information derived from the sample may be subject to a speculative search on the NDNAD.

4.59 It has been reported that up to 40 per cent of people who voluntarily provide elimination samples also consent to having their sample stored permanently and their profile loaded onto the NDNAD where it will be used in speculative searches for the indefinite future.[37] If this is true, we believe such a level of consent might be lower if the consent were fully informed and properly considered. It more likely reflects the stressful experience of being involved in a crime and its investigation. No volunteer samples were loaded onto the NDNAD before 2004–05, yet during 2004–05, 12,095 samples were loaded, and a further 3,953 in 2005–06.[38]

4.60 The House of Commons Science and Technology Committee report of 2005, *Forensic Science on*

36. Rawley A and Caddy B (2007) *Damilola Taylor: An independent review of forensic examination of evidence by the Forensic Science Service* (London: Home Office).
37. Joan Ryan MP, House of Commons, Hansard, 9 October 2006, column 492W.
38. Mr Sutcliffe MP, House of Commons, Hansard, 9 May 2006, column 209W.

Trial, stated that "We do not understand why consent should be irrevocable for individuals who are giving DNA samples on a voluntary basis".[39] The Government response explained that:

> "The rationale for not permitting a volunteer to withdraw their consent… is to avoid a return to the situation prior to the Criminal Justice Act 2001. Situations where consent had been given and then withdrawn, but for whatever reasons the profile remained on the database and was found to match that taken from a crime scene, could lead to arguments as to the admissibility of such evidence in any subsequent criminal proceedings. Withdrawal of consent could also be a precursor to future illegal activity."[40]

This irrevocability is at odds with consent to retention in other contexts, such as medical research, and seems to have been included only for reasons of practical convenience to NDNAD users. As we note in paragraph 3.12, if an individual wishes to withdraw their consent, but is not permitted to do so, their consent can no longer be seen as a moral justification for what would otherwise be an invasion of their privacy.

4.61 The permanent retention of samples from victims, witnesses and those invited to volunteer samples was criticised by many respondents to our consultation. The lack of evidence on the efficacy of keeping volunteer samples, and the potential risks and impact upon privacy, lead to questions of necessity and proportionality, and the benefits of keeping such bioinformation 'just in case'. There should also be special consideration when the consent is given by a minor, with an appropriate adult countersigning the consent form. There is a particularly strong case that the minor should be able to revoke the earlier consent upon reaching adulthood. Such considerations also pertain to mentally impaired adults.

4.62 **It is our view that consent given by a volunteer to retain their biological samples and resulting profile on the NDNAD must be revocable at any time and without any requirement to give a reason. This is a basic principle in all medical research and should equally apply to the voluntary component of the NDNAD, as it already does to the Scottish DNA Database. In view of the importance of this principle, we recommend that as a matter of policy, volunteers should not be asked to consent to the permanent storage of elimination biological samples and retention of DNA profiles derived from these samples beyond the conclusion of the relevant case.**

Equal treatment: black ethnic minorities

4.63 Attention has focused on the over-representation of members of black ethnic groups (at least as far as can be inferred from the 'ethnic appearance code' that accompanies profile records; see Box 1.3 and paragraphs 6.12–6.17) and the number of young persons (under 18) without criminal records on bioinformation databases. As at November 2006, there were 98,707 black males aged 15–24 on the NDNAD. Approximately 75 per cent of the NDNAD is comprised of profiles from white European individuals. Seven per cent of profiles are from 'Afro-Caribbean' individuals, compared with the three per cent proportion of Afro-Caribbean in the general population. Latest figures on the proportion of profiles on the NDNAD versus representation in the community suggest that one third of young black males are on the NDNAD, as compared with one eighth of young white males. Particular attention has been drawn to the numbers of 'non-white' samples retained from individuals who have not been convicted of an offence. In London, 55 per cent of the total number of innocent people on the NDNAD are black or Asian, while 29 per cent of the London population are black or Asian.[41]

4.64 A variety of views were expressed by consultation respondents on the significance of the

39. House of Commons Science and Technology Select Committee (2005) *Forensic Science on Trial*, paragraph 75.

40. UK Government (2005) *Forensic Science on Trial: Government Response*, p7.

41. John Reid MP, 11 June 2007, Written Answers, column 894W.

number of individuals from black ethnic minority groups on bioinformation databases. It is acknowledged that the disproportion is a reflection of police arrest practices and there is dispute over the fairness of those practices and the significance of the resulting over-representation of black ethnic groups. Some argue that the issue cannot be addressed by considering bioinformation collections in isolation from other issues shaping police practices in making arrests, while others believe that their disproportionate representation on such databases may further undermine black ethnic minority confidence in the justice system and diminish their chances of fair and equal treatment. It seems likely that the proposed retention of profiles and samples from all arrestees will further exacerbate these skewed proportions (see paragraph 4.21). This raises issues about equal treatment, as outlined in paragraphs 3.14–3.16. As mentioned there, the NDNAD Strategy Board has commissioned an Equality Impact Assessment of police sampling and 'all policies and procedures relating to the NDNAD'.

4.65 The Home Affairs Select Committee has recently expressed concern about the disproportionate numbers of young black males on the NDNAD. In its report *Young Black People and the Criminal Justice System* (June 2007), it is stated that:

> "It appears that we are moving unwittingly towards a situation where the majority of the black population will have their data stored on the DNA database. A larger proportion of innocent young black people will be held on the database than for other ethnicities given the small number of arrests which lead to convictions and the high arrest rate of young black people relative to young people of other ethnicities... It means that young black people who have committed no crime are far more likely to be on the database than young white people. It also means that young white criminals who have never been arrested are more likely to get away with crimes because they are not on the database. It is hard to see how either outcome can be justified on grounds of equity or of public confidence in the criminal justice system."[42]

The Report goes on to recommend further research: "to determine the implications of so many black males being present on the NDNAD".[43]

4.66 **In our view, the disproportionate over-representation of black ethnic minorities on the NDNAD is a matter of considerable concern, even if this arises from policing practice in making arrests rather than a fault with the NDNAD. Such disparities increase the risk of stigmatisation attendant on being known to have a profile on the NDNAD and can potentially lead to further alienation of whole ethnic communities. We therefore welcome the commissioning of an equality impact assessment by the NDNAD. This assessment should reveal the extent to which it is the discretionary use of powers of arrest or the use of sampling powers that contributes to over-representation of black ethnic minorities. The NDNAD and police forces will then be under a positive obligation to take effective steps to address this over-representation.[44] As we pointed out in paragraph 3.16, the promotion of equality of opportunity entails active steps to remove any practices that unjustifiably cause disparities between different groups.**

Children and young persons

4.67 While it is unsurprising that young people are over-represented on forensic databases in light of the peak age of offending, this has provoked criticism. Young people feature predominantly in

42. Home Affairs Select Committee (2006) *Young Black People and the Criminal Justice System*, paragraph 33.

43. *Ibid.*, paragraph 319.

44. Race Relations Act 1976, as amended, s.71 and Sched.1A, paragraphs 55–60.

arrest statistics, with 330,800 arrests of 10 to 17-year-olds made in 2004/05 (although this is not the total number of minors arrested as some will be arrested more than once during the year), resulting in 195,483 disposals (a penalty or other conclusion of the case).[45] In 44 per cent of these cases, the disposal was by a reprimand or final warning, given to juveniles to try to keep them out of the criminal justice system. The Home Office estimate that about four per cent of 10 to 17-year-olds are arrested per year: just under a quarter of a million, and yet around half of arrests of juveniles do not lead to any finding of guilt, or any further action being taken.[46] Such statistics are important when considering the impact of the proposed changes by the Home Office to permit sampling of all those arrested (see paragraph 4.7). This would clearly encompass many juveniles, many of whom were actively being kept out of the criminal process, or whose arrest did not lead to any criminal proceedings.

4.68 Recent campaigns have highlighted the inclusion on bioinformation databases of children and young persons.[47] Statistics such as those below have prompted critical media attention:

- a total of 512,901 samples have been loaded onto the NDNAD, since its inception, from individuals aged under 16 at the time of sampling;[48]
- in October 2005, 741,605 of the 3,466,792 subject sample profiles retained on the NDNAD at that time related to people who were under 18 when their sample was obtained;[49]
- approximately two per cent of the subject samples presently on the NDNAD are from individuals sampled when they were under 14;[50]
- in December 2005 it was estimated that about 24,000 of the records on the NDNAD related to persons who were under 18 when their samples were obtained and against whom no further action was taken.[51]

4.69 The pattern of arrests, where no further action was taken, is reflected by the numbers of minors on the NDNAD who had not been charged or convicted of any offence. On 1 December 2005, there were 24,168 persons under 18 on the NDNAD who had not been charged or cautioned for any offence.[52] As of 1 February 2006, 541 of those 24,168 profiles had been matched to DNA recovered from unresolved crime scenes.[53] A further 27,000 persons on the NDNAD who had not been charged or cautioned for any offence were under 18 years of age at the time they were arrested and had a DNA sample taken but had reached 18 by 1 December 2005.[54] An unknown additional number will have been acquitted by a court.[55]

4.70 It may be argued that retaining bioinformation from young people is contrary to Article 40 of the UN Convention on the Rights of the Child, in that the Convention requires special attention to be given to the treatment of children by legal systems, to protect them from

45. Home Office (2005) *Arrests for Recorded Crime (Notifiable Offences) and the Operation of Certain Police Powers under PACE 21/05 England and Wales, 2004/05*, Table AB, p3, available at: http://www.homeoffice.gov.uk/rds/pdfs05/hosb2105.pdf, accessed on: 13 July 2007.

46. Home Office (2006) *Young People and Crime: Findings from the 2005 Offending, Crime and Justice Survey*, Table 4a, p48, available at: www.homeoffice.gov.uk/rds/pdfs06/hosb1706.pdf, accessed on: 13 July 2007.

47. For example, campaigns by 'ARCH' – Action on Rights for Children; GeneWatch UK; www.leavethemkidsalone.com; and Privacy International.

48. House of Commons, Hansard, 10 May 2007, column 430W.

49. National DNA Database (2007) *The National DNA Database Annual Report 2005–2006*, p33.

50. *Ibid.*, p33.

51. *Ibid.*, p33.

52. National DNA Database (2007) *The National DNA Database Annual Report 2005–2006*, p33.

53. Joint response to our consultation on behalf of the Association of Police Authorities, the Association of Chief Police Officers and the Home Office.

54. Written answer to a Parliamentary question by Hazel Blears, 2 May 2006.

55. At the end of 2005, there were about 200,300 people who had been acquitted but had their DNA profiles retained on the NDNAD. An unknown number of these were under 18. National DNA Database (2007) *The National DNA Database Annual Report 2005–2006*, p32.

stigma, and that if they have offended, opportunities for rehabilitation to be maximised. The destruction of relevant criminal justice records and accompanying body samples could comprise one element in such a rehabilitative process. At the same time, the Home Office and ACPO argue that sampling young offenders is useful because of their greater likelihood to go on and have extended criminal careers. This is supported by research in the United Kingdom using data from the British Offenders Index, which shows that the most significant variable in predicting length of criminal career is a first conviction before the age of 14.[56]

4.71 In our view, the policy of permanently retaining the bioinformation of minors is particularly sensitive in the United Kingdom, where the age of criminal responsibility is low (at age ten years in England and Wales and eight in Scotland) compared with many other countries. There is a separate youth justice system, in recognition of the special protections that should be afforded to children and young persons. The European Convention on Human Rights recognises the special case of children in the criminal justice system. The Supreme Court of Canada, while acknowledging the strong public interest in crime detection, has held that it was contrary to principles of the youth justice system to treat juveniles in the same way as adults, and that juvenile immaturity was a factor which militated against inclusion on the database.[57] Parental consent for sampling would not, in our view, negate concerns surrounding the retention of samples and profiles of minors.

4.72 **When considering requests for the removal of profiles from the NDNAD and the destruction of biological samples taken from minors (including from adults who were minors when the DNA was taken), we recommend that there should be a presumption in favour of the removal of all records, fingerprints and DNA profiles, and the destruction of samples. In deciding whether or not the presumption has been rebutted, account should be taken of factors such as:**

- **the seriousness of offence;**
- **previous arrests;**
- **the outcome of the arrest;**
- **the likelihood of this individual re-offending;**
- **the danger to the public; and**
- **any other special circumstances.**

A population-wide database?

4.73 The Home Office has proposed that there should be an extension of police powers to take bioinformation without consent from individuals arrested in connection with non-recordable offences (see paragraph 4.21), but it appears unlikely that powers will extend to taking samples from individuals before the point of arrest in the near future. Nevertheless, there is recurrent public discussion of the potential for a comprehensive DNA database holding the profiles of all the population. The recent proposal that fingerprints be used as a biometric identifier on the planned United Kingdom Identity Register may pave the way for the later inclusion of DNA profiles on such a universal register. As a population-wide identification tool, DNA profiles suffer two disadvantages. Current technology does not allow a person's DNA profile to be determined in real time as a check on their identity. If this were to become possible, identical twins (almost one per cent of the population) have identical DNA profiles,

56. Francis B, Soothill K and Piquero A (2007) *Estimation issues and generational changes in modelling criminal career length Crime and Delinquency* **53**: 84–105.

57. *R v RC* [2005] 3 SCR 99 (Supreme Court of Canada).

but not identical fingerprints, making fingerprints the more obvious choice for a population-wide database for instant identification checks, should one be introduced.

4.74 There was a sharp division of opinion on this issue among respondents to our consultation. Some argued that the contribution to crime control and public safety would justify the financial investment and offer a proportionate benefit to any loss of privacy. Respondents also proposed a compulsory population-wide database as the solution to discrimination and inequalities in treatment. For example, Benedict Birnberg, who has over 40 years experience as a civil liberties lawyer, argues that: "A universal bioinformation database [...] would remove the taint of discriminatory selection, of some people being stigmatised because their bioinformation and not others was held [...]. There would remain some potential for bioinformation being put to sinister use but that potential would be reduced by being held by an independent repository." Indeed, the creation of an independent body, instead of the police, to hold the NDNAD has been suggested as a solution to many of the concerns highlighted in this Report and independence of oversight, in particular, is a critical issue that should be addressed in any consideration of the NDNAD (see Chapter 7).

4.75 There was equally strong support among consultation respondents, however, for the view that such databases should only hold information on those who had been proved to have committed criminal acts. Notwithstanding the proposed inclusion of fingerprints on the Identity Register, the joint response to our consultation from the Association of Police Authorities, ACPO and the Home Office argued that "It would be difficult to justify taking DNA and fingerprints from the majority of the population who do not come into contact with the criminal justice system if only on grounds of cost", adding that there were (unspecified) "additional ethical and practical issues". Even the use of existing blood-spot cards (which hold a drop of blood taken from a heel prick in every newborn) to compile such a database would be extremely expensive.[58] It may also be expected that parental consent for these 'Guthrie spots' would diminish if their use was to be extended to inclusion in forensic databases, and such a proposal does not account for practical or logistical difficulties, including issues of tracing individuals decades after their birth.

4.76 Drawing on our discussions in Chapter 3, we note that it would be compatible with a rights-based approach to accept a certain degree of intrusion into the individual liberty and privacy of all if this were necessary in order to avoid unacceptable discrimination. However, rights advocates could also argue that a population-wide database raises questions about proportionality: the increased risk to civil liberties would be compensated by only a negligible increase in public safety. In addition, there are also broader concerns that such a development would significantly shift the relationship between the individual and the state insofar as it treats all individuals as potential offenders rather than as citizens of good will and benign intent.

4.77 There is little reason to believe that the establishment of a population-wide database would in itself prevent discrimination in policing practice (e.g. in arrests and in taking samples) against certain vulnerable groups. A more effective way of countering discrimination is through changes in policing practice towards these groups (see paragraphs 4.63–4.66 for specific recommendations). There would also be increased dangers from 'function creep' (paragraphs 6.19–6.21), given that a population database would be a much more attractive resource to a wide variety of organisations, agencies and corporations. The security of such

58. In any event, as an important general policy, NHS services should not be diverted to this sort of purpose. It may be argued that if people cannot trust Guthrie card information to be used solely for the health benefit of their child, they may start refusing to allow the sample to be taken. This would have both personal and public financial consequences for children requiring lifelong institutional care because phenylketonuria and other illnesses had not been diagnosed at an age at which they could have been treated.

a database would be vital as 'leakages' could have very serious implications. Concerns about logistics and the accuracy of the data would be magnified with a database covering over 60 million people. Linkages with other databases would also become far more complex (see Chapter 7), with a number of ramifications to be considered and perhaps protected against, including the implications of a treaty permitting EU-wide access.

4.78 Further, the NDNAD was created to be a forensic database, specifically concerned with collecting data from what the police describe as the 'active criminal population', for no other reason than forensic purposes (or identification of the dead). There would be a need for far more wide-ranging and intensive public debate if a database were to be established which would extend its remit beyond this group (although some argue that it has already extended beyond active criminals) or beyond forensic purposes. Even those who believe in social solidarity and community obligations may object to a population-wide database on the grounds that, although assisting crime control, it would be seen as a significant step towards an unacceptable 'surveillance society'.

4.79 **Currently, the balance of argument and evidence presented to us is against the establishment of a population-wide forensic DNA database. We conclude that such a response would be:**

- **disproportionate to the need to control crime;**
- **unlikely to secure public support; and**
- **impractical for the collection of samples from different categories of persons (such as visitors to the United Kingdom).**

However, the possibility of its establishment should be subject to review as biometric technology develops, and in the light of research on the potential contribution of such a database, under appropriate safeguards, to public safety and the detection of crime, and its potential for reducing discriminatory practices.

Chapter 5

Trial

Trial

Introduction

5.1 This chapter considers the use of bioinformation evidence after a police investigation, when the decision to prosecute a suspect has been taken. The 'matching' of a fingerprint or biological sample found at a crime scene with a suspect will have an impact upon decision making at the charging stage of the criminal process, and such evidence will be used to support the progress of a case to trial, and at the trial. Forensic bioinformation evidence cannot be considered infallible (if only because of the involvement of humans), and a fingerprint or DNA 'match' alone will rarely be conclusive evidence of guilt. Therefore, care needs to be taken over the use of forensic bioinformation evidence throughout the criminal process, including during prosecutions.

Pre-trial considerations

5.2 Forensic bioinformation matches (see Box 4.2 on police terminology) can be influential in determining the progress of a case and whether a prosecution will proceed. Police and solicitors have reported to us that the positive matching of a fingerprint or biological sample found at a crime scene with a suspect can persuade many defendants to plead guilty (and indeed legal advisers to recommend this). Early guilty pleas clearly save time and money for the criminal justice system. However, sound evidence of such savings, supported by statistics, is not yet available. Care must be taken to ensure that suspects are not placed under undue pressure to plead guilty when faced with forensic bioinformation evidence, as it may be inconclusive. Such evidence requires careful interpretation in the context of the case as a whole, and it may be wrong to assume guilt on the basis of this evidence alone.

5.3 In some instances, a 'match' will be very powerful evidence of guilt, whereas in others it may prove of little relevance or value in assisting a prosecution (for example when the identity of the defendant is not an issue in the case). In many cases there may be an innocent explanation for the presence of a defendant's fingerprint or DNA at the scene of a crime. The strength (or 'probative value') of fingerprint or DNA 'match' evidence thus depends upon the circumstances of each case and should not automatically lead to a decision to prosecute. Indeed, the Crown Prosecution Service (CPS) guidelines clearly state that a DNA 'match' cannot be the sole basis of a prosecution.[1]

5.4 The CPS has introduced a 'staged reporting' process (see paragraph 4.30), whereby cases can be 'speeded up' where there is DNA evidence. Staged reporting is designed to minimise unnecessary work and delays by focusing on the matters relevant to the case in question. For example, where rape is alleged, but the issue is one of consent as the defendant does not deny sexual intercourse, there is no need for a full evaluative statement dealing with the identity of the defendant. By writing to the defence legal advisor early in the prosecution process, the prosecution identifies the issues in the case that are to be disputed by the defence. Such an approach aims to establish whether any significant issues rest on the scientific evidence. If so, the CPS then assesses whether the DNA evidence requires 'full evaluative analysis' (a full report by a forensic scientist) rather than simply the documentation indicating an initial 'match' made by a computer.

5.5 Since the launch of this 'speeded up' approach, time and cost savings have been claimed by the CPS although it concedes that an accurate measure of financial and time savings is not possible.

1. *Guidance for Cases Involving DNA: Processing DNA Samples for Abbreviated and Full Evaluative Statements – Staged Reporting*. This guidance updates the Prosecution Team DNA Guidance issued in August 2004.

However, the CPS has stated that in 2005/06 the Forensic Science Service (one of the providers of DNA analysis for the National DNA Database (NDNAD)) received 1,887 requests for an abbreviated statement reporting an initial match (cost approximately £100), which were followed by 175 further requests for a complex or full evaluative statement (cost approximately £600). Prior to the staged reporting process, all 1,887 requests would have been for the more expensive evaluative statements (approximate cost £1,132,200) yet the abbreviated statements cost approximately £293,700, saving £838,500 (or a 74 per cent saving).[2] (This of course presumes that full evaluative statements would actually have been pursued in all of these cases.) An abbreviated statement is also much more quickly produced, freeing time in the laboratory. It is claimed that the application of this approach to a greater variety of cases would further save time and money, but take-up of the approach has, to date, not been universal across all police areas.

Defence and disclosure difficulties

5.6 In order that a defendant has the opportunity to challenge a fingerprint or DNA match, or its interpretation, it is vital that all DNA and fingerprint evidence is disclosed (in a timely manner) to the parties. Several miscarriages of justice have highlighted the problem of non-disclosure of evidence to the defence. It is essential that, when a prosecution case relies upon a fingerprint or DNA match, the defence parties have the ability to examine this evidence and subject it to their own analysis and interpretation. Defence experts may have many tasks, including:

- Verifying prosecution evidence and undertaking further tests if necessary. (However, there are often obstacles to re-testing as it is rare for there to be disputes between scientists, and the necessity of re-testing must be shown. There may be resistance to the borrowing of notes or facilities and samples, with priority given to the prosecution. Finally, costs of testing for the defence may be prohibitive.)
- Clarifying findings and interpretations of prosecution evidence (often to overcome the lack of scientific understanding on the part of the lawyers involved).
- Advising the defence legal team on how to challenge the prosecution case.
- Providing testimony on an alternative finding or interpretation of evidence.[3]

It is, however, expensive to employ an independent expert to examine prosecution fingerprint or DNA evidence or to do re-testing (and can add considerable delay). Prior authority from the Legal Services Commission[4] is needed for the costs to be recovered, and budgetary demands mean that approval for such expenditure is rarely given unless there is some positive evidence pointing away from guilt.

5.7 Full and timely disclosure is essential so that decisions can be made as to the need for an independent expert. There remains concern over whether all experts appreciate their duty to the court to disclose any material that might undermine the prosecution case or assist the defence case. Following revelations of serious cases of non-disclosure, in particular of experts' reports, steps have been taken to provide advice to experts involved in criminal proceedings, as well as the establishment of a general disclosure regime since the passing of the Criminal Procedure and Investigations Act 1996.

5.8 Nevertheless, there remains some contention over which information must be disclosed. Moreover, the disclosure regime is highly discretionary and does not demand the disclosure of

2. National DNA Database (2007) *The National DNA Database Annual Report 2005–2006*, p10.
3. Roberts P (1994) Science in the criminal process *Oxford Journal of Legal Studies* **14:** 496–506.
4. The Legal Services Commission is responsible for legal aid in England and Wales. A similar requirement applies to payments from the Scottish Legal Aid Board.

preliminary reports, which may reveal scientific dispute or disagreement at an early stage of testing procedures, instead disclosing only the final, consensus report. The evidence of an earlier dispute or disagreement over a match may be important to a defence case, and a simple match report may not prove sufficient as the basis for constructing the defence case if this precludes critical assessment of the DNA evidence. Our fact-finding meetings revealed that some experts believed that differences of opinion that had been expressed in a laboratory were not disclosable, and that the defence would be required to seek out any details of disputes that may have an impact upon the certainty with which evidence can be approached. The scope of the obligation to disclose relevant and unused material is therefore in need of clarification.

5.9 **We recommend:**

- **Compulsory and timely disclosure of *all* fingerprint bureau or DNA laboratory results and relevant records to all parties involved, including details of any dispute over an identification, rather than presenting only the consensus view reached.**
- **In expert witness statements and reports, this duty of disclosure should be explicitly acknowledged and the experts should confirm that they have complied with this duty.**

Forensic bioinformation evidence at trial

5.10 In research studying the impact of DNA evidence on trials in Australia, it was found not only that cases with DNA evidence were more likely to reach court, but also that DNA evidence (and incriminating fingerprints) assumed great strength in influencing jury decisions, with juries 33 times more likely to convict where prosecutors produced DNA evidence.[5] In a US study, the presence of DNA evidence resulted in a variance in sentencing severity, with DNA convictions leading to harsher sentences.[6] The authors concluded that "one inescapable fact remains: DNA testimony is already having a significant, if little understood, impact on rendering justice in serious felony cases".[7] If bioinformation evidence is similarly persuasive in England and Wales, and such impacts are also occurring in English and Welsh courts,[8] it makes it vital that bioinformation evidence is properly presented in court, and fully understood by juries and legal professionals alike, to prevent miscarriages of justice.

5.11 Although the reliability of fingerprint comparison is under increasing scrutiny, and the standard for fingerprint match reporting changed significantly in 2001 (see paragraphs 2.4 and 5.14), fingerprint evidence is very rarely ruled inadmissible at trial. In the case of forensic DNA evidence, in early cases in the late 1980s and early 1990s, the courts questioned the reliability and validity of this new evidence, but initial challenges have been resolved (in tandem with advances in science and technology which have removed much ambiguity, see paragraphs 2.9–2.14). Currently there is an expectation of admissibility, unless the defence can present a strong argument against the admission of the evidence. Despite such a presumption in favour of admitting DNA evidence, there remain some issues of potential concern. In particular, the accurate presentation of complex scientific and statistical information to a non-scientific audience (which of course includes most of the legal profession as well as the jury) can be particularly difficult.

5. Briody M (2002) The effects of DNA evidence on sexual offence cases in court *Current Issues in Criminal Justice* **14(2)**: 159–81, 170; Briody M (2004) The effects of DNA evidence on homicide cases in court *Australian and New Zealand Journal of Criminology* **37(2)**: 231–52.
6. Purcell N, Thomas-Winfree L and Mays G (1994) DNA Evidence and Criminal Trials: An exploratory survey of factors associated with the use of 'genetic fingerprinting' in felony prosecutions *Journal of Criminal Justice* **22(2)**: 145–57, 153.
7. Purcell N, Thomas-Winfree L and Mays G (1994) DNA Evidence and Criminal Trials: An exploratory survey of factors associated with the use of 'genetic fingerprinting' in felony prosecutions *Journal of Criminal Justice* **22(2)**: 145–57, 156.
8. It may be that this is of less concern in Scottish Courts, where there is a legal requirement for corroboration of all evidence.

5.12 It is almost impossible to comprehensively eradicate the potential for confusion among the legal professionals (barristers, judges, magistrates, court clerks, etc.) and jury members, as well as the defendant, victims and members of the public. What can be properly inferred from forensic bioinformation evidence may be either exaggerated or understated by those who are called upon to make a judgment based upon such technical evidence. Popular media representations of the power of fingerprint or DNA evidence may exacerbate such difficulties in courtrooms.

Presenting scientific evidence

5.13 At trial, forensic scientists are afforded special privilege in being able to give evidence of their opinions as well as fact. Their opinions can prove highly persuasive, making informed cross-examination of expert testimony vital. Those forensic scientists called upon to testify at trial clearly began their work on the case in question far earlier in the criminal process and may have carried out their analysis many months previously. Scientists are required to report on testing undertaken by the laboratory staff for whom they are responsible, and therefore present the results of tests that they did not perform themselves. It will most often be the final conclusions that will be presented, and any doubts or disagreements between scientists may not be reported. However, it may also be easy for advocates to give the impression that there is a dispute between experts where the real difference may simply be down to a choice of words. Where there is genuine scientific dispute, the limitations of the adversarial system, and in particular the courtroom as a site for resolving such dispute, can be magnified, and calling upon juries to decide upon guilt where there is scientific disagreement has the potential to lead to injustice.

5.14 As a result of the ruling in *R v Buckley*,[9] it has become clear that fingerprint evidence can no longer be presented in court as if it were a simple statement of fact that there is a match between a crime scene mark and an accused person's print. Expert evidence that identifies marks linking an accused person to a scene of crime is evidence of opinion based on examination of the materials using the skill and experience of the expert. It is important to remember that Judge Rose RJ ruled in *R v Buckley* that:

> "In every case where fingerprint evidence is admitted, it will be generally necessary, as in relation to all expert evidence, for the judge to warn the jury that it is evidence of opinion only, that the expert's evidence is not conclusive and that it is for the jury to determine whether guilt is proved in the light of all the evidence."

5.15 Thus fingerprint evidence should be presented in a similar way to the presentation of handwriting evidence, for example. However, fingerprint officers continue to assert that if three experts agree on a match then it is a '100% correct' match. Such a conclusion may not in fact be justifiable in the light of the change to a non-numerical standard in June 2001 (see paragraph 2.4). **We recommend that in presenting their opinion regarding a positive match or otherwise to the investigating officer, prosecution authority or court, fingerprint experts should make it clear that their conclusion is always one of expert judgment, and never a matter of absolute scientific certainty.**

Presenting DNA evidence

5.16 It is vital that DNA evidence is properly interpreted within the particular circumstances of the case, and not represented as providing definitive evidence of guilt. The weight to be given to DNA evidence and its presentation at trial were considered in *R v Doheny and Adams*.[10] A DNA

9. *R v Buckley* (1999) 163 JP 561.

10. *R v Doheny & Adams* [1997] 1 Cr. App. R. 369; see also Crim LR [1997] 669.

expert in *Doheny* testified that it was his opinion that the offender was the defendant. The trial judge directed the jury that if this evidence was to be believed, guilt had been conclusively proved. This was contrary to the proper interpretation of the DNA evidence, that whilst there was a very small group of other people that could match the DNA profile, the defendant was only one of this small group. In *R v Adams* (Gary), both the expert and prosecutor at this trial had committed the prosecutor's fallacy (see Box 5.1), though this did not invalidate the verdict because the defendant had also been positively identified by the victim. However, the Court of Appeal ruled that it was vital, in light of the increasing use of DNA evidence, that the profiling process be understood and that the manner in which the evidence is presented be made as clear as possible. There were two opposing views on the best way of presenting DNA evidence:

- reporting how rare the profile was in the population (known as the 'random occurrence ratio'); and
- reporting that, given the match of the DNA profile from the crime scene with that from the suspect, then, if the sample had come from someone other than (and unrelated to) the defendant, the probability of obtaining such a match was, for example, one in a million.

The Court of Appeal ruled in favour of the reporting the rarity of the profile in the population (the random occurrence ratio).

5.17 The Court of Appeal also set out guidelines to minimise the risk of misuse of DNA evidence including:

- any issue should be identified and resolved before trial in pre-trial review;
- the expert witness should not be asked his or her opinion on the likelihood that it was the defendant who left the crime stain, nor when giving evidence should he or she use terminology that may lead the jury to believe that he or she was expressing such an opinion; and
- it was inappropriate for an expert witness to expound a statistical approach for evaluating the likelihood that the defendant left the crime stain, because unnecessary theory and complexity divert the jury from their proper task.

5.18 The decision in *Doheny and (Gary) Adams* has not always been adhered to and there still remains confusion in some cases (see the Privy Council case of *R v Pringle*).[11] In the case of *R v Bates*,[12] there was a thorough examination of issues arising in cases where only a partial DNA profile was found at the crime scene, and yet the interpretation of the judgment itself was still subject to some confusion.[13] Such confusion surrounding statistics and their presentation and interpretation in court has been clearly highlighted in recent 'cot death' cases.

5.19 The Royal Statistical Society (RSS) has taken an interest in this area following its interventions in recent cases where statistics have been misrepresented during trials. The RSS became involved in the case of Sally Clark, who was convicted of murdering her two baby sons. In court, a paediatrician miscalculated the probability of two instances of sudden infant death syndrome (SIDS) occurring in the same family as 1 in 73 million. This statistic was used as evidence during the trial, as well as being widely reported outside the courtroom, despite being seriously flawed. The RSS expressed its concern in the media, and wrote directly to the Lord Chancellor, commenting:

> "Aside from its invalidity, figures such as the 1 in 73 million are very easily misinterpreted. Some press reports at the time stated that this was the chance that the deaths of Sally Clark's

11. *R v Pringle* [2003] UKPC 9.
12. *R v Bates* [2006] Crim EWCA 1395.
13. For a critical appraisal, see Cooke G (2007) More twists in the DNA saga *Archbold News* **9**: 2 November, p4.

> two children were accidental. This (mis-)interpretation is a serious error of logic known as the Prosecutor's Fallacy. The jury needs to weigh up two competing explanations for the babies' deaths: SIDS or murder. Two deaths by SIDS or two murders are each quite unlikely, but one has apparently happened in this case. What matters is the relative likelihood of the deaths under each explanation, not just how unlikely they are under one explanation (in this case SIDS, according to the evidence as presented). The Court of Appeal has recognised these dangers ... in connection with probabilities used for DNA profile evidence, and has put in place clear guidelines for the presentation of such evidence. The dangers extend more widely, and there is a real possibility that without proper guidance, and well-informed presentation, frequency estimates presented in court could be misinterpreted by the jury in ways that are very prejudicial to defendants."[14]

The RSS subsequently formed a working party on statistics and the law, to address some of the main issues. The working party has yet to report its findings and recommendations, which may be of relevance in cases involving DNA evidence.

Box 5.1: The prosecutor's fallacy

Debate concerning the precise definition of the 'prosecutor's fallacy' can become highly technical. The expression was first used by Thompson and Schumann, who described the problem:

> "The fallacy in the prosecutor's logic can best be seen if we apply his analysis to a different problem. Suppose you are asked to judge the probability a man is a lawyer based on the fact he owns a briefcase. Let us assume all lawyers own a briefcase but only one person in ten in the general population owns a briefcase. Following the prosecutor's logic, you would jump to the conclusion that there is a 90 per cent chance the man is a lawyer. But this conclusion is obviously wrong. We know that the number of nonlawyers is many times greater than the number of lawyers. Hence, lawyers are probably outnumbered by briefcase owners who are not lawyers (and a given briefcase owner is more likely to be a nonlawyer than a lawyer). To draw conclusions about the probability the man is a lawyer based on the fact he owns a briefcase, we must consider not just the incidence rate of briefcase ownership, but also the a priori likelihood of being a lawyer. Similarly, to draw conclusions about the probability a criminal suspect is guilty based on evidence of a 'match,' we must consider not just the percentage of people who would match but also the a priori likelihood that the defendant in question is guilty."[15]

For our purposes, we consider that the prosecutor's fallacy is committed whenever the recipient of the statistical evidence, upon hearing the evidence, believes that they have been told the likelihood of guilt or innocence which can then be considered without any reference to the prior likelihood of the defendant being guilty or innocent. This arises when the rarity of a particular profile (or the 'match probability' as many scientists call it) is presented as being interchangeable with the probability that the defendant is innocent, such that, for example, a profile with a rarity of 'one in a million' produces the false conclusion in the mind of the recipient of the evidence, that the chance of the defendant being innocent is 'one in a million'.

'One in a million' means that, in a country of, for example, 60 million people, there will be approximately 60 people with that profile. Without other evidence, the defendant is then no more likely than the other 59 with the same profile to be the actual offender. Looked at this way, the probability of guilt, not innocence, is about one in 60. Other evidence may, of course, change that probability.

If there is a full SGM+ match of the suspect's DNA and that recovered from a crime scene, then the rarity is expressed as 'of the order of one in a billion'. Even though this is very powerful evidence it does not by itself prove conclusively that the defendant was the source of the crime scene profile. There is still the possibility that somebody else (especially a close relative) may have the same profile.

5.20 The prosecutor's fallacy has bedevilled the use of DNA evidence in courts. It tends to take the form that the frequency of the occurrence of the profile in the population is described as a probability of occurrence and then this is taken to be the 'chance' of innocence. Arguably, the continued use of the 'match probability' wording rather than the 'rarity' or 'frequency' approach, can be said to contribute to the difficulties. Even though the 'match probability' wording does not, in itself, commit the prosecutor's fallacy, it tends to be widely misunderstood among the public, and poor reporting by journalists can perpetuate the confusion.

14. The full media release can be found at www.rss.org.uk (accessed on: 13 July 2007), Royal Statistical Society (2001) *Royal Statistical Society concerned by issues raised in Sally Clark* case, 23 October.
15. Thompson WC and Schumann EL (1987) Interpretation of statistical evidence in criminal trials: the Prosecutor's Fallacy and the Defense Attorney's Fallacy *Law and Human Behavior* **11(3)**: 167–87, 170.

5.21 The courts further considered the weight of DNA evidence in the cases of *R v Watters*[16] and *R v Mitchell.*[17] Watters was originally convicted of four burglaries based solely on a DNA match from cigarette butts found at the scene of burglaries, the prosecution relying upon the similarity of the burglaries to claim the same people had been responsible for each. The prosecution also relied on facts that the defendant was a smoker, lived locally and was male. The appellant argued that the DNA evidence was weak (there was only a partial profile giving a match probability of 1 in 79,000), and additionally that the defendant had a brother – which reduced the match probability further to 1 in 267. The DNA expert claimed that the DNA evidence should not have been used in isolation as this in itself did not constitute proof. The Court of Appeal concluded that the case should not have been put before a jury because of the confusion over the brothers (the other brother was also suspected of being in the burglary team). If the jury were not able to determine decisively that the defendant was guilty (and that, for example, it was not his brother who was the guilty party) then all the jury could do was acquit.

5.22 In *R v Mitchell* the appellant successfully argued that the fact that DNA swabs taken from the victim (which had been deposited by the perpetrator of the crime) did not match his DNA profile strongly supported his defence of mistaken identity. The trial judge had summed up at his trial that the DNA evidence was entirely neutral and could not assist the jury. The Court of Appeal disagreed, finding that a 'non-match' could indeed be powerful evidence in favour of the accused, which the jury should consider. The Court concluded that when considering DNA evidence, judges should take great care not to raise scientific speculative possibilities and so detract from evidence that the defence could rely upon.

5.23 Concerns over the presentation of DNA evidence are increased when considering the use of DNA analysis techniques that go beyond the standard methods of SGM+ profiling typically used (see Box 2.2). For example, there are differing views expressed by scientists and the forensic DNA analysis providers on the use of low copy number (LCN) techniques used when only very tiny amounts of DNA can be recovered from a crime scene (see paragraphs 2.30–2.31). Concerns about this technique focus upon the heightened possibility of contamination when very small amounts of material are amplified to obtain a profile. As an illustration, a scientist explained that LCN testing used in the following situation could be problematic: a doorknob is touched with a bare hand and that doorknob is later touched by a gloved hand, which then is used to handle an exhibit; DNA left on the doorknob by the first person could thus be present on the exhibit despite the fact that the first person had never come into contact with that exhibit.

5.24 While the technology enables a DNA profile to be obtained from a fraction of a nanogram (a billionth of a gram) of DNA, the possibility of contamination that could be given inappropriate significance is also greatly increased. The results may therefore be misleading, and yet they could be presented as powerful evidence in a courtroom. This makes it vital that defendants are not convicted on a DNA match alone. Crown Prosecutors must decide in their professional opinion at what point, in each case, there is sufficient corroborative evidence to proceed with a prosecution. In *R v Smith,*[18] Smith's appeal after conviction was rejected although the DNA match left him a suspect along with 43 other men in the United Kingdom, because there was also quite clearly evidence of him having been arrested after the offence a short distance away. However, such a ruling may raise a risk that individuals could be charged with a serious criminal offence on the basis of a circumstantial association with the crime scene represented by a DNA match between their DNA and biological material recovered from such a scene. Such a possibility is even more likely where techniques such as LCN DNA analysis are used (see Box 2.2).

16. CA (Criminal Division) unreported, 19 October 2000.

17. *The Times*, 8 July 2004.

18. *R v Smith* CA 9904098 W3 (8 February 2000).

5.25 The use of DNA analysis by LCN may be an example where the science has progressed further than the ability of courts to handle it properly, courtrooms being inappropriate sites for the resolution of scientific debates. Indeed, one important test of the admissibility of expert evidence is whether the science or technique has been peer-reviewed and is 'accepted' by the scientific community. It has been made clear to us that there remains significant scientific debate over the reliability of this technique, which should preclude its admissibility in courts until such a time as it is accepted by the forensic DNA community.

5.26 A DNA match should therefore only be used as circumstantial evidence pointing towards the guilt of the defendant. In the leading case of *Teper v R*,[19] the judge explained to the jury that they were permitted to infer the accused's guilt from circumstantial evidence as long as they were sure that there were no other co-existing circumstances that would weaken or destroy the inference. Usually, the inference suggested by the prosecution will be that there are few (or very few) people with a matching DNA profile and that there is other evidence consistent with the defendant being the perpetrator. The magistrates, or jury, will have to take account of other evidence – for example alibi evidence (or lack of it), differences in any description of the offender and the character of the defendant – and decide whether on all the evidence they can be sure of guilt.

Difficulties with scientific evidence

5.27 To be credible in court, experts must be not only expert in their field, but must also be expert in presenting evidence. However, it cannot be ruled out that jurors, as well as others in the courtroom, will have difficulty in following scientific evidence, while experts in court, just as in life outside the courtroom, can exert a great deal of influence, or can be partisan. Expert witnesses are explicitly under a duty to report to the court, and are not to present their evidence in such a way as to favour either the defence or prosecution case. Whether it is the prosecution or the defence that has instructed them to testify should therefore have no bearing on their evidence, although in reality this neutrality has not always been achieved.

5.28 Research has pointed to a series of possible problems with the level of understanding by the jury, including 'white coat syndrome', which is where the jury members are of the opinion that evidence can only be understood and 'disentangled' by experts. Further, there are language difficulties, with the nature and meaning of terms such as DNA requiring explanation. Jurors are required to enter the realms of both genetics and statistics, with some likely to be "unduly influenced by overtly probabilistic evidence because it exudes an 'aura of precision'".[20] Researchers in Australia note:

> "[T]he interpretation of DNA evidence requires expertise from several fields, notably genetics, statistics, laboratory technique, and crime-scene analysis. On a number of occasions, Australian courts have permitted a person qualified in a single field to present an opinion based on several fields."[21]

This phenomenon of experts testifying on areas beyond their expertise has been widely reported in the courts in England and Wales (for example, toxicologists testifying as to the cause of death, and see paragraph 5.19, where a paediatrician testified on statistics; indeed the RSS assert that only trained statisticians should be permitted to provide statistical evidence).

5.29 Researchers have also found that jurors have "high expectations for the significance of DNA

---

19. *Teper v R* [1952] A.C. 480 at 489.

20. Schklar J and Diamond S (1999) Juror reactions to DNA evidence: errors and expectancies *Law and Human Behaviour* **23(2):** 159–84, 160.

21. Gans J and Ubas G (2002) DNA identification in the criminal justice system, in *Trends and Issues in Crime and Criminal Justice*, No. 226 (Canberra: Australian Institute of Criminology), p4.

evidence. This may be based more on popular culture rather than scientific understanding. Such disproportionate expectations can produce frustration ... but overall did not significantly diminish the jurors' belief in the probative importance of DNA."[22] This problem is exaggerated by the trend to incorporate DNA as an essential feature of prosecutions, the DNA evidence represented as 'compelling', with jurors' expectations of DNA "compounded through media representations of DNA as conclusive proof of a person's guilt".[23] In England and Wales, the law prohibits inquiries into jury deliberations so we can only use 'mock juries' to gauge how juries assess DNA evidence (or any evidence for that matter).

5.30 There are, however, reported examples of misunderstandings by judges, lawyers, police officers, journalists and even some forensic scientists. For example, we were informed by an accreditation body for forensic practitioners that it had previously discovered a forensic laboratory that was committing the prosecutor's fallacy in its written reports. While this and other flaws in their written reports may not have led directly to a miscarriage of justice, it clearly highlights failures in the oversight of forensic practitioners and laboratories. Training of forensic practitioners must address such issues to ensure that the highest standards are reached and maintained. A code of conduct should apply to all scientists working in forensic laboratories, and a commitment made to transparency, both of the operation of forensic laboratories and scientists, but also their accrediting bodies. Such transparency is fundamental to the fairness of the criminal process, with any concerns about forensic science standards in a particular case revealed to all parties.

5.31 It is therefore legitimate to assume that if scientists can make mistakes both inside and outside courtrooms, jurors may be making mistakes during their secret deliberations. In *R v Denis Adams*,[24] the Court of Appeal rejected the argument that the complexity of evidence was a ground upon which DNA evidence could be excluded. However, the Court ordered a retrial because the use by the defence of Bayes theorem (a logical method of weighing up different pieces of evidence) had: "plunged the jury into inappropriate and unnecessary realms of theory and complexity deflecting them from their proper tasks".

5.32 Respondents to our public consultation felt that juries required some preparation for weighing up evidence in the form of bioinformation, and that it should not be assumed that members of the public could readily understand the complexities of the science and statistics involved. It is the correct presentation of technical evidence that is critical to jurors' understanding and the proper carriage of justice. In recent observations during research undertaken in Australia, it was found that trial advocates were prone to misrepresenting the significance of DNA evidence, which then influenced juries.[25] However, preconceptions of jurors, largely determined by representations of forensic DNA evidence in popular culture, were found to have as great an impact upon the jury understanding of evidence as the actual presentation of the evidence to them during the trial. Most jurors expected the DNA evidence to be very significant prior to its presentation in court.

5.33 Such high expectations of the significance of forensic bioinformation makes essential the proper education of legal professionals, throughout the criminal justice system, to prevent the misrepresentation of evidence, or at least to ensure the recognition of flawed evidence or of the misrepresentation of evidence when it is presented. It also highlights the need for a thorough, transparent and stringent accreditation and oversight body for forensic practitioners, as well as for laboratories (see Chapter 7 for recommendations concerning governance issues).

---

22. Findlay M and Grix J (2003) Challenging forensic evidence? Observations on the use of DNA in certain criminal trials *Current Issues in Criminal Justice* **14(3)**: 269–82, 282.

23. *Ibid.*, p274.

24. *R v Denis Adams* [1996] 2 Cr. App. R. 467 see also J of CL (1997) 61(2) 170 and Crim LR [1996] 898.

25. Findlay M (2007) Juror comprehension and the hard case – making forensic evidence simpler, *International Journal of the Sociology of Law*, forthcoming.

5.34 **In view of the difficulties with the presentation of complex statistical information in the courtroom, we recommend:**

- **that professionals (including judges) working within the criminal justice system should acquire a minimum standard of understanding of statistics, particularly with regard to DNA evidence;**
- **that trial judges ensure statistical evidence is accurately presented during trials, and that the decision in the *R v Doheny and (Gary) Adams* (1997) 1 Cr. App. R. 369 judgment regarding the correct presentation of DNA evidence is adhered to; and**
- **that in all cases where bioinformation evidence is adduced, introductory information should be made available to jury members, to ensure some basic understanding of the capabilities, and also the limitations, of such evidence.**

Chapter 6

Familial searching, inferring ethnicity and research uses

Familial searching, inferring ethnicity and research uses

Introduction

6.1 In this chapter we consider the expansion of uses of the National DNA Database (NDNAD). When the Database was first established, it was limited in its use to the matching of DNA profiles with crime scene samples. As the Database grew, speculative searching could be undertaken. With the massive growth of the Database, the uses to which the DNA profiles, and indeed the retained biological samples, can be put have expanded.

6.2 The Police and Criminal Evidence Act 1984 makes clear that police bioinformation databases may only be used for:

- the prevention or detection of crime;
- the investigation of an offence;
- the conduct of a prosecution; or
- identifying a deceased person or a body part.

It precludes their use in medical or other research, or in paternity disputes.[1] Such terms, however, may be subject to a wide interpretation that expands the range of uses to which the information on the databases may legitimately be put. While, to date, forensic databases have been used primarily to 'match' known suspects with crime scenes, they are increasingly used in efforts to identify unknown suspects: by searching the NDNAD for possible relatives of a perpetrator, or for predicting the likely ethnic appearance of an unidentified suspect, for example.

6.3 While most of the uses of the NDNAD can be classified as 'operational', in that the use is directly related to particular police investigations, there are now emerging 'research' uses of the Database. Research could be conducted using the electronic records ('profiles') on the Database or the archived biological samples from which the DNA profiles have been generated. In considering research uses it is therefore important to distinguish between these. The House of Commons Science and Technology Committee has noted that biological samples have already been used for research and has recommended that independent studies be undertaken on public attitudes to this.[2]

6.4 Expanding use of the NDNAD beyond operational uses makes crucial the need to introduce robust forms of ethical oversight and management of these uses, particularly in instances where the research uses the archived biological samples. These samples contain sensitive personal genetic information and their use warrants stricter regulatory oversight. Advanced levels of ethical and scientific review are necessary as these samples are not initially obtained with consent, unlike those collected in medical settings, and remain easily traceable to named individuals. This chapter first considers 'operational' uses of the NDNAD before turning attention to broader 'research' uses of the Database and stored biological samples.

1. *Lambeth London Borough Council (Applicant) v (1) S (2) C (3) V (4) J (By his children's guardian N) (Respondents) and (1) Commissioner of Police of the Metropolis (2) Secretary of State for the Home Department (Intervenors) (2006)* [2006] EWHC 326 (Fam).
2. House of Commons Science and Technology Select Committee (2005) *Forensic Science on Trial*, paragraph 87.

Operational use of the NDNAD profiles and biological samples

Quality assurance

6.5 We note that the use of the NDNAD to improve operational performance and DNA analysis procedures, and to guarantee the quality of the Database itself, is non-contentious. Compulsory quality assurance procedures include re-analysing a proportion (usually five to ten per cent) of randomly selected biological samples to check laboratory error rates. This can provide statistics on the performance of the NDNAD that may be used to identify weaknesses. Whilst this may be an acceptable use of both data and samples, there is a lack of transparency about the exact nature of such projects, making it difficult to assess how, or if, this statistical research might be related to other research that has been concurrently undertaken (see Chapter 7 on transparency). The use of the NDNAD for 'quality assurance' is now classified as 'routine management information' and not deemed research.

Familial searching

6.6 When a crime scene profile does not match any stored profile, it is possible to undertake further testing to see if it partially matches any of those held on the NDNAD. Such a partial match might mean that the crime scene stain was left by a (genetic) relative of the person to whom the partial match is made. The Forensic Science Service (FSS) Forensic Intelligence Bureau first offered this 'familial searching' service to support the investigation of some serious crimes, and other forensic providers now also perform the service.[3] Familial searches can only be conducted with the specific authority of the Custodian of the NDNAD (see Chapter 7). Home Office statistics state that 73 familial searches were undertaken in 2004, 78 in 2005[4], and 115 in 2006.[5] As explained in paragraph 2.16, the search is likely to produce very many possible partial matches. This severely limits the usefulness of familial searching. The size of the pool must be limited geographically and/or by other means to produce a useful shortlist for police, to be investigated using standard police methods.

6.7 The Association of Chief Police Officers (ACPO), the Home Office, the Information Commissioner, and representatives from the Human Genetics Commission have agreed upon the circumstances in which familial searches will be performed and the confidential results integrated into an investigation. However, the details of this agreement are described as 'operationally sensitive'. It is not a public document and has not been disclosed to our Working Group.

6.8 Many respondents to our consultation remain seriously concerned about whether familial searching is an unjustifiable intrusion into personal privacy, given its potential to reveal family secrets (see Box 6.1). There is a clear need to maintain strict protocols relating to the use of familial searching and the confidentiality of information derived from the process. However, the public have yet to be reassured that appropriate safeguards are in place. In the scenarios detailed in Box 6.1, the risks of revealing unknown biological relations, or the absence of relations where they are presumed, are relatively small. Although this is highly sensitive information, and 'Mr X' may not wish to find out from the police who his biological father is (assuming he did not already know), whether this is indeed revealed depends upon the degree of confidentiality with which the police treat this information. The public fear of revelation of family 'secrets' may therefore be more to do with the heightened sensitivity of the issues than the actual risk posed.

3. The Forensic Science Service has considered the utility of such extended database searches since 1996 after an internal paper on 'near-misses'. Some of this work arose from efforts to deal with 'close-relative defences'. (See for example Evett I (1992) Evaluating DNA profiles in a case where the defence is "it was my brother" *Journal of the Forensic Science Society* **32(1)**: 5–14).

4. Mr Sutcliffe, House of Commons, Hansard, 9 May 2006, column 209W.

5. Written Answer to Parliamentary Question from Norman Baker, 17 January 2007.

Box 6.1: Familial searching – scenarios

Suppose Mr X left his DNA at a crime scene. He may be the criminal or there may be an innocent explanation; either way the police want to identify him as part of their enquiries. They obtain a DNA profile from the crime scene and search the NDNAD. No match is found. They then use familial searching to see if any profile on the NDNAD might come from one of Mr X's relatives.

Note that a partial match would not prove that an identified person is Mr X's relative, or even make it highly probable. For example, paternity testing as done for family courts relies for its accuracy on having DNA from the mother as well as the alleged father.

In this hypothetical case the familial search brings up two possible hits, Mr A and Mr B. Mr A and Mr B are asked to provide names and addresses of any sons (for example). The names are given and each son is asked to provide a biological sample. Now we imagine two circumstances where there is a family secret:

Case 1: Mr X is in fact an illegitimate son of Mr A. If Mr A chooses to reveal this secret to the police, Mr X will be tested and any court case (if there is one) will rely on the match between Mr X's DNA and the crime scene profile. If Mr A does not reveal the secret, or maybe is unaware of it, Mr X will not be on the list of sons he provided to the police, so will not be tested. Even if Mr X is later identified through some independent line of enquiry, there would be no reason to link him to Mr A. The only way the relationship would become known to the police is by Mr A volunteering this information. The only way the paternal relationship would then be revealed to Mr X would be if the police were to reveal the secret. However, there is a possible risk that the police might reveal this information if Mr X sought the grounds upon which he was being asked for his DNA.

Case 2: Unknown to both, Mr B is not the biological father of his son Y. In that case Y's DNA profile will bear no relation to Mr B's profile, and hence no relation to Mr X's profile. Having been eliminated from the enquiry, Y is of no further interest. Laboratories do not report the actual marker alleles that make up the profile; the report will state that there is no match between Y's profile and that obtained from the crime scene. At no time will any report or analysis list the actual alleles of Y's and Mr B's profiles alongside one another, so that the incompatibility might be noticed.

Case 2, for example, suggests that the practice of profile comparison underlying familial searching might not always pose the substantial risk that may be presumed from initial consideration of the technique. The risk of directly making public information that particular family members either do not wish the police or others to know, or do not themselves already know, may be small if the police were to handle their inquiries and the information derived from them with the utmost diligence and integrity. Not only do the police need to be careful how they approach the persons whose profiles are on the NDNAD and their possible relatives, but also adhere stringently to the principle that any information about genetic relatedness (or its absence) remains entirely confidential to the relevant scientific and investigative teams.

6.9 Some respondents to the consultation were also concerned that familial searching may be carried out for 'non-forensic' uses, either by individuals who wish to capitalise on information about the existence of biological relations between individuals, and/or employees of agencies, institutions or organisations (such as the Family Court, social workers or the Child Support Agency) who may wish to establish paternity or other familial relations. It should be reiterated that it has been affirmed that it would be illegal for the Family Court to compel police to reveal information from forensic biological samples to assist with paternity inquiries as this was not a purpose described in the Police and Criminal Evidence Act 1984.

6.10 The legal parameters for use of the NDNAD are clearly delineated: the prevention and detection of crime, the investigation of an offence, the conduct of a prosecution – or the identification of a deceased person. This affords some certainty about how the NDNAD may be lawfully used, in that it is clear that it cannot be used in paternity, or other disputes. However, in light of public concerns about the use of familial searching, further information on how it is being used operationally and clear accountability are required. It is also imperative that whatever guidelines do exist be compared with actual practice, particularly because it is recognised that the consequences of any resulting police inquiries may resonate widely within the family and the community for some time after initial inquiries are made, especially after media attention or when a criminal case proceeds to court.

6.11 The aim of familial searching may be to provide legitimately useful intelligence in crime solving and there may be instances in which its use is able to be justified and is proportionate (for example, tracing the male relatives of an unidentified serial killer may be deemed a justifiable intrusion into familial relations). However, before the technique is implemented on a wide scale, public fears should be recognised by introducing clear and explicit guidelines on its use and these should be made available for scrutiny. In light of the potential for familial searching to reveal previously unknown or concealed genetic relationships, and for publicly revealing a relationship with an offender, there must be adequate safeguards to protect against any possible unwarranted intrusion into family privacy. **While we do not believe that familial searching interferes with privacy rights to an extent that should prohibit its use (see paragraphs 3.3–3.7), it is our view that the potential benefits for crime detection must be balanced carefully with any potential for harm. The lack of consent obtained when sampling makes the use of the NDNAD in searching for relatives particularly sensitive. It is important therefore that this technique is not used unless it is necessary and proportionate in a particular case. Before it is more widely deployed, there needs to be detailed and independent research on its operational usefulness and on the practical consequences for those affected by it.**

Inferring ethnicity

6.12 The inferring of ethnicity is a statistical process that can be applied to a particular DNA profile, with the aim of predicting the 'ethnic appearance' of the unidentified individual to whom the DNA profile relates (see paragraph 2.17 and Box 6.2). The NDNAD (unlike the Scottish DNA Database) contains information on an individual's 'ethnic appearance'. This is based on visual judgments made by police officers about those from whom they are taking a biological sample, or on that person's invited self-classification. Police officers routinely classify suspects into one of seven categories for recording, statistical and other purposes throughout the criminal process. These 'ethnic appearance' categories, as recorded on the PNC are:

- Afro-Caribbean
- Arab
- Asian
- Dark Skinned European
- Oriental
- White Skinned European
- Other.

6.13 These generalised and subjective categories may help police officers communicate with each other, but they do not correspond with the types of classification used in population genetics research. A police officer's perceived assignment may also not accord with a self-assignment. As Cho and Sankar[6] have illustrated, the use of such labels varies greatly over space and time, and in some groups they are rarely applied, even by the individuals themselves, with any consistency. In biological terms, human beings are one undifferentiated species. Visible differentiations in skin colour or other characteristics are the product of complex interrelationships between genetic factors, as well as environmental and social factors that are highly variable: for example skin colour may be influenced by extent of exposure to sunlight. Thus apparent ethnicity may not be well predicted by reference to a relatively small set of short tandem repeat (STR) loci.

6.14 The FSS and other forensic suppliers offer to make inferences about an offender's likely ethnicity from crime scene DNA profiles, such inferences being based upon calculations arising from research previously undertaken on a sample of NDNAD profiles. Results for an individual will, however, in general be limited because the chain of inference between DNA profile and ethnic appearance is long, and every link is loose:

- The different alleles of markers in the SGM+ profile appear with different frequencies in different ethnic groups, but the frequencies are statistical properties of groups, not individuals. All alleles can be found in all groups.

6. Cho M and Sankar P (2004) Forensic genetics and ethical, legal and social implications beyond the clinic *Nature Genetics* **36**: S8–12.

- Ethnicity can rarely be accurately summed up by a single label or category.
- The seven ethnic appearance categories are not straightforwardly related to actual ethnic origin.
- Ethnicity is often only loosely linked to actual appearance.

6.15 Our public consultation revealed considerable concern about the use of DNA profiles to make ethnic inferences, and about research into this area (Box 6.2). This centred upon the flawed assumption that it is possible to assign accurately and consistently a 'racial type' both to individuals and to the population groups against which their identity can be compared. Behind the concerns may lie an anxiety that the classification of people into seven 'ethnic appearances' may seem closer to racist ideas than to genetic understanding of ethnicity, and that the research is seen by some people as attempting to lay a scientific foundation for racial categorisation. Much mainstream genetic research is indeed devoted to exploring the differences between human populations and making inferences about ancestry. However, the results of genetic research do not support the idea that humans can be classified by appearance into a limited number of 'races'.

Box 6.2: Ethnicity research using forensic DNA

Information on the perceived ethnicity of offenders has been used to undertake several research projects using DNA collected for forensic use in recent years. At least five requests have been made to access either stored biological samples or DNA profiles (we do not know which) with the intention of analysing them for research into markers of ethnicity. Since 2003 three such requests have been approved. No evidence is available for requests of this nature made before 2001. In 2004 it was reported that the police were requesting ethnic inferences after two Forensic Science Service (FSS) scientists had published research on the use of DNA profiles for inferring the ethnic origin of the donor of a crime scene stain based on studies undertaken on data and profiles stored on the NDNAD. Other projects have been undertaken by scientists at the FSS that seek to predict ethnicity on the basis of frequencies of Y-chromosome haplotypes (combinations of marker alleles that are inherited largely unchanged through the male line). These have been widely used in anthropological research to give information on male ancestry. Research into regional genetic variations has also been undertaken by the FSS. This has extended analysis to a consideration of the existence of genetic variations between particular ethnic groups located in specific regions. It is not known whether this research used DNA profiles or the original biological samples.

6.16 Ethnicity tests provide only an inference for use during a police investigation and are not used as evidence supportive of the prosecution if the suspected offender is found.[7] The information can be used to help reduce a 'suspect pool' and inform police priorities, and may support or contradict any witness statements reporting that the offender had a specified ethnic appearance. Although an ethnic inference may have no prosecutorial power, significant ethical and practical concerns remain. Making an ethnic inference may lead police to narrow the focus of their enquiries prematurely in expectation that the offender will come from a particular racial or ethnic group (referred to as 'tunnel vision').[8] Such tunnel vision has been implicated in subsequent miscarriages of justice. It may also reinforce existing prejudices about the likely perpetrators of crime and support generalisations about the supposed 'predisposition to crime' of populations based upon conclusions of research conducted on small and arguably 'skewed' samples.

6.17 **In view of the significant ethical and practical problems, and the limited usefulness of the information provided, attempts to infer ethnicity from DNA profiles and samples fail the test of proportionality and we recommend that ethnic inferences should not be routinely sought, and should be used with great caution.**

7. National DNA Database (2006) *The National DNA Database Annual Report 2004–2005*, p35.
8. See McCartney C (2005) The DNA Expansion Programme and criminal detection *British Journal of Criminology*, for the risks of 'tunnel vision' in police investigations using DNA; and Duster T (2006) Explaining differential trust of DNA forensic technology: grounded assessment or inexplicable paranoia? *Journal of Law, Medicine & Ethics* **34(2)**: 293–300 for an assessment of the racial implications of the use of DNA 'dragnets' in the USA.

6.18 Some further research in this area may be legitimate and ethically neutral. It may be unobjectionable to use anonymised profiles from the NDNAD to explore whether a predictor of the reported ethnic appearance could be developed. On the other hand, as we discuss further in paragraphs 6.41–6.43, it would be improper for researchers to use NDNAD data to investigate supposed racial propensities to crime.

Non-operational research use of the NDNAD and biological samples

Non-operational research and function creep

6.19 'Function' or 'mission' creep occurs when a project or mission is expanded beyond its original goals. In the case of forensic bioinformation databases this could be evidenced by the expansion of databases to include constituencies that were not originally intended as targets, and by extending the uses to which the databases can be put. For example, DNA profiling was originally introduced to help identify criminals who left retrievable biological material such as blood, semen, saliva and hair at crime scenes (or on victims or witnesses). These were, typically, violent criminals and sex offenders. Forensic bioinformation databases have now been extended to include not only individuals convicted of relatively minor offences but also arrestees, volunteers and others who are innocent of involvement in crime. These developments raise concerns that we are witnessing 'function creep', concerns articulated by Sir Alec Jeffreys, who pioneered DNA fingerprinting:

> "The real concern I have ... is with what I see as a sort of mission creep. When the database was initially established it was to database DNA from criminals so that if they re-offended they could be picked up. There are now hundreds of thousands of entirely innocent people now populating that database, people who have come to the police's attention as a result of being charged with a crime but subsequently released. My view is that that is discriminatory."[9]

6.20 Although less attention has been drawn to the use of the NDNAD for non-operational research, the issues it raises are disquieting. Research on DNA profiles and archived biological samples has extended the uses to which the NDNAD is put. The attractiveness of the NDNAD as a source of data for researchers, such as behavioural geneticists, is likely to make it the subject of further research interest. The imperative to find new ways of reducing offending offers a compelling rationale for governments to allow such research. As has been noted, "the history of fingerprinting [has] demonstrated that criminal identification databases are powerful resources subject to political manoeuvres that can quickly push them beyond their original mandates – the well-established and growing interest in behavioural genetics may contribute to these manoeuvrings".[10] The need to ensure that all research uses of the NDNAD are subject to rigorous ethical review and independent monitoring cannot be overstated.

6.21 Research using the NDNAD should be specifically for the purposes of criminal investigation and detection – i.e. for operational reasons – and non-operational research use could constitute a very broad, and some could argue inappropriately wide, interpretation of that remit. The present criteria for using the bioinformation stored are the "prevention or detection of crime, the investigation of an offence, or the conduct of a prosecution", criteria that can be construed widely. **We make a general recommendation that all research proposals using the NDNAD and stored samples should be formally, independently and transparently evaluated.**

9. BBC Radio 4, *Today* programme, 1 November 2006.

10. Sankar P (2001) DNA-Typing: Galton's Eugenic Dream Realized?, in *Documenting Individual Identity* Caplan J and Torpey J (Editors) (Princeton University Press), pp273–90, pp286–7.

Openness and public scrutiny

6.22 Potential research on DNA profiles or samples is limited by the Police and Criminal Evidence Act (PACE) 1984 to that which is related to the prevention and detection of crime. In deciding upon granting permission for research using data on the NDNAD, the Strategy Board considers whether there is a police need for the purpose for which access is requested, and the legality and ethical aspects of the purpose. In March 2004, Home Office Minister Hazel Blears reported that only five requests to undertake research projects on the NDNAD had been received, of which two had been approved by the NDNAD Strategy Board, two rejected and one was yet to be decided.[11] These requests were decided in the absence of the kind of detailed information about the nature of the projects that would now routinely accompany similar requests to other like biobanks in the United Kingdom (see Chapter 7).

6.23 Since this reporting of research requests, the number has rapidly increased. A list of research proposals put to the NDNAD Strategy Board prior to December 2006, indicates that 33 requests had been made to conduct research, of which 19 were approved and 14 refused. The information provided in the table released by the NDNAD Strategy Board is cursory, however.[12] There are instances in which the principal investigator remains unidentified or where the status of the research is unknown. In all cases only the most perfunctory description of the research is offered (usually just a title) and it is not possible to establish with any certainty the purpose of the research. It is also difficult to determine whether requests are being made to meet police operational needs or as part of a wider research agenda.

6.24 The table provided by the NDNAD Strategy Board shows that six requests have been approved (two operational and four research-based) to obtain *identifying* information about individual profiles on the NDNAD. Several others were disallowed. It is not clear what information was sought (whether relating to individuals or groups) or for what purpose. The first of the two approved operational requests was made by police to check for 'named individuals', but it is not clear what this might mean. Further clarification was provided which explained that such requests related to "seeking named suspects in a specific inquiry at the police's request". This is still far from explaining such a use of the NDNAD. If the police seek a DNA match on the NDNAD and one is found, then that individual's name will be readily known by the police. If the police sought a named individual's DNA profile for purposes other than making a match to one found at a crime scene, this might signal a departure from the purposes for which the NDNAD may be lawfully used. It remains far from clear what the results were of these research requests.

6.25 **At present, there is a significant lack of transparency concerning research using the NDNAD and stored samples, with the cursory details provided in the NDNAD Annual Report being inadequate. Given this lack of information, it is not possible for the public to be reassured that research projects will only be approved if their potential benefits are sufficient to outweigh the harm to the other interests involved. We recommend the regular publication of further details concerning, as a minimum:**

- **information on requests and approvals, including the criteria used to determine approval or refusal;**
- **whether there was informed consent for the use of biological samples;**
- **which individuals have been given approval to undertake research projects using the NDNAD and stored samples;**
- **exactly what the purpose of this research was;**

11. Hazel Blears MP, House of Commons, Hansard, 17 March 2004, column 345W.
12. National DNA Database (2007) *The National DNA Database Annual Report* 2005–2006, p43.

- **whether the research has been subject to adequate levels of scientific and ethical review; and**
- **the outcomes of research.**

Regulation of research using forensic bioinformation

6.26 Since the passage into law of the Human Tissue Act in 2004, it has become a requirement that researchers who approach 'biobanks' or large DNA databases with requests to access their stored informational or biological resources for medical, epidemiological, sociological or other research purposes have their proposals subject to detailed ethical and scientific review, with documentation placed either in the public domain or made available under a Freedom of Information request. This documentation typically involves submitting to the custodian of the bank a very detailed set of documentation clearly outlining:

- which samples, data or information they wish to access;
- an explicit and detailed description of the proposed research project;
- the methodologies they intend to employ;
- an assessment of the ethical implications of the research;
- a summation of the staff who will be working on the project;
- the intended outcome of the project including the likely dissemination of published findings and arrangements for public deposition of findings or materials (such as datasets) created from the project which must be updated and reported at the conclusion of the project; and
- a Material Transfer Agreement[13] that legally regulates the parties that may access the required resources and the terms and conditions under which they may do so.

6.27 Forensic providers have explained that up until very recently, access requests took the form of an 'exchange of letters' between the company and the NDNAD Custodian. During 2006 a standardised form was produced which has recently become available for scrutiny. However, it still appears not to offer the level of detail that would ordinarily be required for medical research purposes. Thus, the decision-making body that approves requests for research access, the NDNAD Strategy Board (see paragraphs 7.30–7.32 for details), may have inadequate information to make informed decisions about the scientific worth, ethical robustness, or utility for the police of the research proposals before it.

6.28 Criticism of the lack of proper ethical oversight of research requests prompted a commitment by the Home Office to establish a dedicated Ethics Group in the summer of 2007 (see paragraph 7.19). Such a committee is vital because it cannot otherwise be guaranteed that research is not ill-conceived or poses risks to individuals through inadequate anonymisation, or acts to perpetuate racial or other stereotypes. The new Ethics Group will not be able to discharge its task unless adequate information or documentation is produced on proposed research. This is a priority. It also appears from the documentation that it will be determined by the NDNAD Strategy Board whether or not the Ethics Group will be asked to consider a research proposal – referral to the Group does not appear to be automatic. The Strategy Board could therefore decide not to refer a research proposal to the Ethics Group, or of course could ignore its advice if it so chose. Such decisions and their reasoning should be made publicly available (see Chapter 7).

6.29 At present, The Human Tissue Act (2004) S. 39(1), excludes any activities undertaken 'for criminal

13. A Material Transfer Agreement (MTA) is a contract that governs the transfer of tangible research materials between two organisations, when the recipient intends to use it for his or her own research purposes. The MTA defines the rights of the provider and the recipient with respect to the materials and any derivatives.

justice purposes' from the general remit of the Act. Researchers who wish to access the NDNAD resources are not, therefore, necessarily required to provide the same level of information about their prospective research projects as is demanded of researchers who wish to access other similar tissue banks and bioinformation databases in the United Kingdom.

6.30 It is not clear that a compelling argument can be sustained to support such a broad exception. The practicalities of police work are such that it would be entirely inappropriate to require forces to submit operational requests to detailed ethical and scientific review. It is not evident, however, that non-operational research projects – particularly those that involve ethnicity or genetic behavioural research – should not be subject to the same strict regime of ethical and scientific review now required of all other researchers who undertake similar studies on like collections of archived biological material and bioinformational resources in the United Kingdom.

6.31 **Notwithstanding the fact that the operation of forensic databases falls outside the purview of the Human Tissue Act (2004), we recommend that all research projects involving biological samples collected for forensic use be subject to the same regime of scientific, ethical review and oversight that currently governs access to, and use of, other human biological sample collections in the United Kingdom. This is particularly so in light of the fact that the samples are not sufficiently anonymised (with a link to the datacard still possible after archiving of the sample), and also because none of the individuals whose NDNAD samples are stored has given their consent for their samples to be used for specific research purposes.**

6.32 **Further, we would make it an absolute requirement that any NDNAD samples or data provided for research should be irreversibly anonymised (that is, neither the researchers nor the Custodian or any NDNAD staff should be able to relate any result to any named individual). A condition of the release of any biological sample to researchers should be that the researchers would not profile the DNA of any sample. It would be necessary to ensure that, even if the researchers were to do so, they would never be allowed to interrogate the NDNAD to identify the individual with that profile. If such safeguards could not be put in place for a research project, the project should not be permitted.**

6.33 It has been argued that biological samples should be subject to stricter security and oversight. The Government undertook during the passage of the Criminal Justice and Police Act in 2001 to give consideration to the suggestion that an independent body be given responsibility for the archives of forensic biological samples. Informed debate about how their custodianship should be organised has yet to materialise, just as there has been little public or political debate over the necessity for the retention of all biological samples on the scale now seen (see paragraphs 4.36–4.56). We consider proposals for wider governance reform in the next chapter.

The storage and analysis of DNA by private companies

6.34 The storage and analysis of biological samples is a service that currently three companies provide to police forces[14] although their number is set to rise. Given that biological samples may yield sensitive personal information it is imperative that robust, internationally recognised regulations are in place that prohibit unlawful access to, and unlicensed transfer of, them. Regular audits ensuring that samples or DNA profile databases are not misused are essential (see Chapter 7). **We recommend that organisations and companies that have custody of biological samples complete a standard Material Transfer Agreement, subject to ethical review, that establishes the terms and conditions under which samples may be accessed and used by subsequent recipients.**

6.35 The biological samples stored by private companies remain the property of the police force

14. The Forensic Science Service, LGC Forensics Ltd. and Orchid Cellmark.

that submitted them. The subject samples sent by the police to the private companies are accompanied by the individual's 'datacard', which contains the name of the person from whom the sample was taken, and their gender. This is inconsistent with the method of protecting genetic privacy commonly used in medical and other scientific research, namely to de-link stored biological samples from identifying data so that only a very small number of individuals (ideally custodians) have access to both the samples and the identifying data.

6.36 Private providers of DNA analysis have all commented that they have no need to retain the 'datacard' that is sent with the subject sample to laboratories, which contains the name of the person from whom the sample was taken, and their gender. These cards are not of use to the company, and yet create the possibility that security and confidentiality of samples could be compromised. **We recommend that datacards should not be provided to private companies. Non-coded identifying details (such as a name) should be removed from the sample as early as possible during the DNA analysis and storage process.**

6.37 The provision of DNA analysis by private companies has extended the 'chain of custody' of these biological samples. In addition, the number of providers of DNA analysis is set to increase, stretching present operative and geographic parameters (there is nothing currently to prevent an international company entering the market and, indeed, one of the current providers of DNA analysis has a US parent company). Many of these companies already carry out other genetic analysis for other customers, including the Home Office Immigration Directorate, the Child Support Agency and the Department for Environment, Food and Rural Affairs on the same premises.

6.38 It is clear that the forensic analysis of DNA and the retention of biological samples demands the highest operating standards in terms of security, ethical operations and quality. Such standards must not only be reached but also maintained and closely monitored (see Chapter 7). Private companies will, however, also wish to improve upon their processes and procedures, and expand their business opportunities. This may be done by undertaking research on further possible DNA analysis, or on software to interpret DNA profiles, etc.; research that will often necessitate access to information from the NDNAD.

6.39 Such requests for 'commercial' purposes require particular scrutiny from the NDNAD Strategy Board, to ensure that research which primarily supports the development of a business opportunity does not gain approval unless fulfilling strict criteria. It is not clear that such strict criteria are currently applied. For example, a research request disclosed in the table of research proposals (see paragraph 6.23) provided by the NDNAD Custodian, for 'access to profile data' from a private company, raises particular questions. It is not evident why the company should seek this access and what information this might include. This is of concern for two reasons. First, the record does not indicate whether this request was approved. Second, it is not clear what data protection or security measures were in place to ensure that staff of the private company could not access identifying information on the profile data and samples, and create an opportunity for misuse.

Emerging and future developments in forensic DNA analysis

6.40 There is constant innovation in the technological process of DNA profiling and its uses in support of criminal investigations. The current state of knowledge in these areas is discussed in Chapter 2. Current strands of innovation include:

- methods for the analysis of small and degraded crime scene samples;
- statistical programmes to assist in the interpretation of mixed samples;
- the development of devices for speedier processing of crime scene samples, possibly at the

scene itself;

- the analysis of genetic material to reveal a variety of physical characteristics of the originating person; and
- the identification of genetic relatedness.

The Police Science and Technology Strategy 2003 to 2008 makes a commitment to develop ways to 'predict physical characteristics' from DNA. There are obvious advantages for police in being able to refine a target population of suspects for any crime(s). The current state of the technology gives no indication that it is likely to develop quickly. Nevertheless, use of the NDNAD and the analysis of DNA will continue to be refined.

Genetic behavioural research

6.41 There is ongoing research outside the forensic arena, in the area of behavioural genomics, in which researchers seek to identify genetic sequences which, singly or in combination, and in the presence of certain environmental triggers, can impact upon behaviour. The Council's report *Genetics and Human Behaviour: The ethical context* considered that it would be "neither a theoretical nor a practical impossibility to identify genes that contribute to behavioural traits [or] to consider some of the mechanisms by which they do so".[15] However, we cautioned strongly that it is misleading to present this as research that seeks to establish the existence of 'a gene for x' (in this case criminality). Subsequent research has confirmed this view. The complexity of the relationship between genetic, environmental and social factors in the causation of human behaviour is such that individual genes will only very rarely be directly related to a complex behavioural characteristic. The predictive capabilities of tests for any single or small number of genes will, in general, be quite limited.

6.42 Although the notion of a 'crime gene' is simply wrong, forensic DNA databases may still be of use to behavioural geneticists who wish to explore genetic variations influencing behaviours such as novelty seeking or impulsiveness which some believe are linked to criminal or anti-social conduct. Research of this type may extend to include comparative research by racial or ethnic type, in an effort to establish if those variants implicated in particular behaviours appear more or less frequently among members of particular ethnic or racial groups. Such research could, however, have serious implications, including:

- misleading inferences, taking the presence of a sample on the database as indicative of the commission of an offence, or taking the absence or rarity of samples from certain ethnic groups on the NDNAD as indicating a reduced likelihood of their committing an offence;
- the exaggeration of the ability to identify 'causal' variants, leading individuals known to have them to be pre-judged and excluded from services such as education, employment and insurance;
- social stigmatisation and racial stereotyping promoted by a misguided belief that all members of a group are pre-disposed to criminality; and
- denial of social causes (e.g. poverty and poor education) of some types of crime leading to a hardening of attitudes and the abandonment of social policy initiatives.

6.43 Further considerations make the use of NDNAD samples or profiles undesirable as a source of data for such research. The NDNAD does not represent a scientifically valid source of samples for such research, for a number of reasons including:

- the unrepresentativeness of the samples;

15. Nuffield Council on Bioethics (2002) *Genetics and Human Behaviour: The ethical context.* (London: Nuffield Council), pxxii.

- the lack of informed consent;
- the current weakness of oversight;
- the difficulty of finding an appropriate control group; and
- the problems with conducting research that is based on what appear to be robust but could, in fact, be rather fluid categorisations (i.e. 'drug offenders', or 'South Asian').

Interpreting any results in light of these deficiencies and then making generalisations that may well be given wide media coverage on the basis of them would be highly problematic.

6.44 **While recognising the potential value of research into genetic behavioural traits and ethnicity, in common with all other non-operational research, proposals in these areas must be subject to robust ethical scrutiny. The scientific credibility of the proposed research must be evaluated, examining, for example, the extent to which inherent biases in the National DNA Database may compromise the ability to identify 'causal' relationships between genetics markers and criminal behaviour and hence support misleading conclusions. Such scrutiny would need to balance any potential benefits from the research against the risks of increasing social stigmatisation and racial stereotyping, or a potential detrimental impact upon efforts to rehabilitate offenders.**

Chapter 7

Governance and ethical oversight

Governance and ethical oversight

Introduction

7.1 In this chapter we emphasise the importance of robust ethics and governance oversight of forensic databases, both as a means to protect the liberty, autonomy and privacy of those whose details are recorded on such databases, and also to help engender public trust and confidence in their existence and use as part of a criminal justice system. The potential uses and abuses of forensic databases are considerable. Effective governance helps to ensure not only that their utility is maximised, but also that their potentially harmful effects – such as threatening privacy, undermining social cohesion and aggravating discriminatory practices – are minimised. Good governance can anticipate and respond to new challenges; it is not merely a means to impose sanctions once things go wrong. Moreover, open governance can address suspicion and promote support among the public for an enterprise which, after all, is essentially in the public interest.

7.2 Forensic databases form an integral part of forensic science services as a whole, so discussion must also necessarily consider broader questions about forensic science in the United Kingdom, including the regulation of forensic science in general, the shift in status of the Forensic Science Service (FSS) from a public body to a Government-owned company (GovCo) and the growing private market in forensic science services. A recent Home Office consultation on the need for regulatory reform of the forensic sciences has indicated radical changes to the regulation of forensic sciences in the UK, citing a demand for greater clarity and regulation, and proposing the creation of a new Forensic Regulator.[1]

7.3 This Report has already identified some of the future regulatory challenges for forensic science services. They include the evolution of technological measures and go beyond the current possibilities of the National DNA Database (NDNAD) and IDENT1 fingerprint database, and look to a time when linkage across various types of forensic database might be possible. In governance terms, this requires considerable foresight and the need to establish frameworks that can meet new challenges as they emerge. It is important therefore, not to compartmentalise the issues, but to think more broadly and to consider how the forensic world might look in the future. Such a holistic approach is envisaged by the NDNAD Strategy Board which has reported that the role of the Forensic Regulator will extend to oversight of all forensic databases in due course.[2] Our recommendations anticipate this eventuality.

The private market in forensic science

7.4 The privatisation of the FSS, prompted by the McFarland Review in 2003,[3] has only partly been realised, although plans for a Public Private Partnership remain.[4] The FSS is now run as a profit-seeking private company, with pricing and all services governed by negotiated contracts, as well as material transfer and confidentiality agreements. The creation, and rapid growth, of a private forensics market has resurrected the need for regulation of forensic services and highlighted the challenges for governance.[5]

1. Home Office Consultation Document (2006) *Standard setting and quality regulation in forensic science*, paragraph 7.
2. National DNA Database (2007) *The National DNA Database Annual Report 2005–2006*, p7
3. Home Office (2003) *Review of the Forensic Science Service* (McFarland Report).
4. For general discussion of market forces in forensic sciences, see: Roberts P (1996) What price a free-market in forensic science services? *British Journal of Criminology* **36**: 37–60.
5. Two new requests for accreditation as DNA suppliers were received by the Custodian in 2005–06, see National DNA Database (2007) *The National DNA Database Annual Report 2005–2006*, p18.

Regulatory oversight

7.5 The Royal Commission on Criminal Justice 1993 first recommended the establishment of a Forensic Science Advisory Council to oversee the regulation of forensic science and provide independent and impartial advice on forensic science. The House of Commons Science and Technology Committee in 2005 repeated this recommendation, stating that the Council should be an independent body including representatives of all the major stakeholders, with a remit to review, or commission inspections of, the use of forensic science across the whole of the criminal justice system, and to propose improvements. While acknowledging the 'regulatory gap', the Government still does not consider that a Forensic Science Advisory Council as originally conceived would be effective, and has instead sought to introduce a more limited version to support the role of the Regulator. To assess its alternative proposals, however, it is necessary first to consider what regulation has gone before, to scrutinise what has been suggested broadly, as well as specifically in relation to the NDNAD, and to contemplate the longer term.

Governance arrangements of IDENT1

7.6 The Police Information Technology Organisation (PITO) previously oversaw the development and operation of IDENT1 – the national fingerprint database that has superseded the National Automated Fingerprint Information System (NAFIS). PITO was subsumed by the National Policing Improvement Agency (NPIA) in April 2007. The NPIA aims to align the work of different groups within policing (including those in charge of training, research and information technology) with business change within the police organisation, connecting more closely the 'front end' operations of policing with the 'back end' support and research operations.

7.7 A number of structures are in place to oversee operations and policy. The Identification Programme Board authorises and governs IDENT1 as part of NPIA's Identification Programme. IDENT1 has a Project Board, which is responsible for reporting to the Programme Board on developments and for ensuring that the project is on track and meets the requirements set out by the users. IDENT1 also has a User Board (IUB) drawn from the fingerprint expert community, and a User Liaison Team, made of up of specialists who communicate with users and identify service improvements required, maintaining regular contact with police forces and stakeholders. The Association of Chief Police Officers (ACPO) has a National Fingerprint Board (NFB) which operates within the ACPO Forensic Science portfolio. It has 20 members drawn from the scientific support and fingerprint community, Scotland, Northern Ireland, the Police Standards Unit, and the Home Office Scientific Development Branch. The NPIA will only deal with operational issues. Changes in policy will remain the preserve of ACPO and the Home Office.

7.8 The functioning of IDENT1 may raise concerns surrounding the 'linkages' with not just the Police National Computer (PNC), but other biometric and informational databases in the future. If such linkage were to be permitted (this would require changes to law and policy) then this 'inter-operability' may open up greater possibilities for wrongful or inappropriate access, for intrusive research and for misuse. The increased likelihood of identifiability might lead to greater risk of breaches of privacy, and for mistakes during inputting and transferring of data. At present, however, there is no independent official or body charged with oversight of this resource or such linkage processes.

7.9 **In our view, IDENT1, like the NDNAD, must retain public confidence in its security, especially its protection from non-authorised access and in control of its uses. This confidence depends on ongoing scrutiny and systematic audit of its uses so that the public can be sure that data held in it are not misused or misrepresented. There should be regular public reports on the use, scrutiny and auditing of this database.**

The National DNA Database

7.10 The FSS provides all operational services for the NDNAD. This contract will be reviewed in 2008 but the criteria for review have not yet been made public. Formerly, the FSS was the standard-setting body for forensic science and maintained an oversight function with respect to the NDNAD in tandem with the Custodian based in the Home Office. Since privatisation, however, the role of the Custodian has been separated from the FSS to ensure that it stays in the public sector.

7.11 The NDNAD Custodian and his staff were formerly located in the Home Office but also moved to NPIA as of 1 April 2007. The Custodian Unit is responsible for overseeing delivery of NDNAD operations and the Standards of Performance for forensic science laboratories. The Custodian is entrusted with maintaining and safeguarding the integrity of the NDNAD and developing policy. Currently, three private organisations and four police laboratories are approved to provide DNA profiles from criminal justice and/or crime scene samples to the NDNAD.[6] While the Council for the Registration of Forensic Practitioners (CRFP) accredits individual forensic practitioners, the UK Accreditation Service (UKAS) accredits laboratories in line with the two major standards: ISO/IEC 17025 and ISO 9000:2000, and the Custodian also has stringent quality criteria and checks. However, there appears to be no formal Inspectorate function to visit and assess the quality of forensic service providers on their own premises or in respect of their handling of samples and other relevant material. The Custodian told us in his reply to our Consultation that he, together with UKAS, continually monitor the performance of laboratories and ensure that any issues are dealt with expeditiously.

7.12 The NDNAD is governed by the NDNAD Strategy Board comprising representatives of the Home Office, ACPO and the Association of Police Authorities (APA). Two members of the Human Genetics Commission (HGC) have a role in providing ethical input in the decision making. The inclusion of ethical representation was prompted by critical reports from the House of Lords Select Committee on Science and Technology in 2001 and the Human Genetics Commission in 2002.[7] The Strategy Board considers that the HGC representatives also provide lay input to the Board.

7.13 The House of Lords Select Committee had expressed concerns about conflicts of interest when the FSS was acting as both user and Custodian of the NDNAD. This was addressed by the removal of the Custodian role from the FSS to the Home Office in 2005, but questions remained about transparency and accountability. The Custodian Unit has now been removed from the Home Office, following the dissolution in 2007 of the 'Forensic Science and Pathology Unit' during a re-organisation of the Home Office, and is now situated within the NPIA. The Royal Commission on Criminal Justice,[8] the House of Lords[9] and the Human Genetics Commission,[10] have all advocated the establishment of an independent oversight body to advise and monitor on the operation of the NDNAD "to put beyond doubt that individuals' data are being properly used and protected".[11] More recently, further criticism

6. Also included are some police forces that have retained 'in-house' forensic departments.
7. House of Lords Science and Technology Select Committee (2001) *Human Genetic Databases: Challenges and opportunities*; Human Genetics Commission (2002) *Inside Information: Balancing interests in the use of personal genetic data*.
8. Royal Commission on Criminal Justice (1993) (Runciman Report) Cm 2263.
9. House of Lords Science and Technology Select Committee (2001) *Human Genetic Databases: Challenges and opportunities*, paragraph 7.66.
10. Human Genetics Commission (2002) *Inside Information: Balancing interests in the use of personal genetic data*, paragraph 25.
11. House of Lords Science and Technology Select Committee (2001) *Human Genetic Databases: Challenges and Opportunities*, paragraph 7.66

from the House of Commons Science and Technology Committee (2005) finally prompted proposals for reform.[12]

7.14 A National DNA Operations Group links the Home Office, ACPO, Scientific Support Managers within police forces, and the DNA suppliers, providing a forum for debate about the operational use of DNA. The Home Office Police Standards Unit also has a remit to ensure that DNA is used to best effect across all police forces. The NDNAD Suppliers Group supplies the DNA Board and Custodian with information relating to scientific standards and strategic developments.[13] This intricate network has meant that there has been no overarching oversight or ethical consideration of forensic services or forensic databases. The Government has stated that it is committed to appropriate ethical review and has established an Ethics Group with a specific remit over the NDNAD.[14] The challenge will be to integrate the work of this body with wider regulation of forensic services more generally.

7.15 The Home Office has further proposed the appointment of a named Regulator – a Quality Adviser for Forensic Science – with personal accountability for a broad oversight remit,[15] who would receive advisory input from a Forensic Science Advisory Council (an idea re-invigorated from the Runciman Commission Report of 1993, see paragraph 7.5), which would include stakeholders in the criminal justice system, members of the scientific community and lay representation. The post would provide an overarching function for approval, monitoring, licensing and enforcement across the range of forensic services, leaving well-functioning sectors intact and intervening where gaps were found. The recommendation is that the individual would be appointed by the Home Secretary with delegated powers, located within the Home Office, report to the Chief Scientific Adviser, and be initially funded by the Home Office. It would be a specific remit of the new Quality Advisor to oversee the operation of the NDNAD.[16] Both the Quality Advisor and the Ethics Group were optimistically reported to be starting work in April 2007.[17] However, this start date has been delayed.

12. House of Lords Science and Technology Select Committee (2005) *Forensic Science on Trial.*

13. National DNA Database (2006) *The National DNA Database Annual Report 2004-2005.*

14. Mr Vernon Coaker, Parliamentary Under-Secretary of State for the Home Department, Parliamentary Statement during debate on the National DNA Database, Hansard, 15 November 2005, column 127.

15. This would include: (1) setting standards for entry to the forensic science market; (2) setting standards for forensic science activities and processes performed by the police; (3) monitoring of compliance with these standards; (4) taking action as required to address shortfalls in performance against standards; (5) oversight and control of forensic science intelligence databases; (6) ensuring that quality standards continue to be assured and improved through development of a contestable and transparent market for forensic science, enabling the entry of new suppliers, with appropriate assurance of continuity of supply; (7) creating an environment where innovation is encouraged, with 'type approval' awarded as appropriate to new techniques or products; (8) identifying, assessing and mitigating potential future risks through modification of regulatory arrangements; (9) supporting public confidence in the contribution of forensic science to the criminal justice system and the reduction of crime and its impact.

16. Response to our consultation on behalf of the Association of Police Authorities, the Association of Chief Police Officers and the Home Office.

17. *Ibid.* An advert appeared in the national press in March 2007 inviting applicants for the Chair and up to eight members of the Ethics Group for the National DNA Database (*The Sunday Times*, 11 March 2007). Membership of the Group was announced in July 2007.

7.16 We understand that the broad architecture of the proposed governance framework for forensic sciences across the industry would, therefore, look like this:

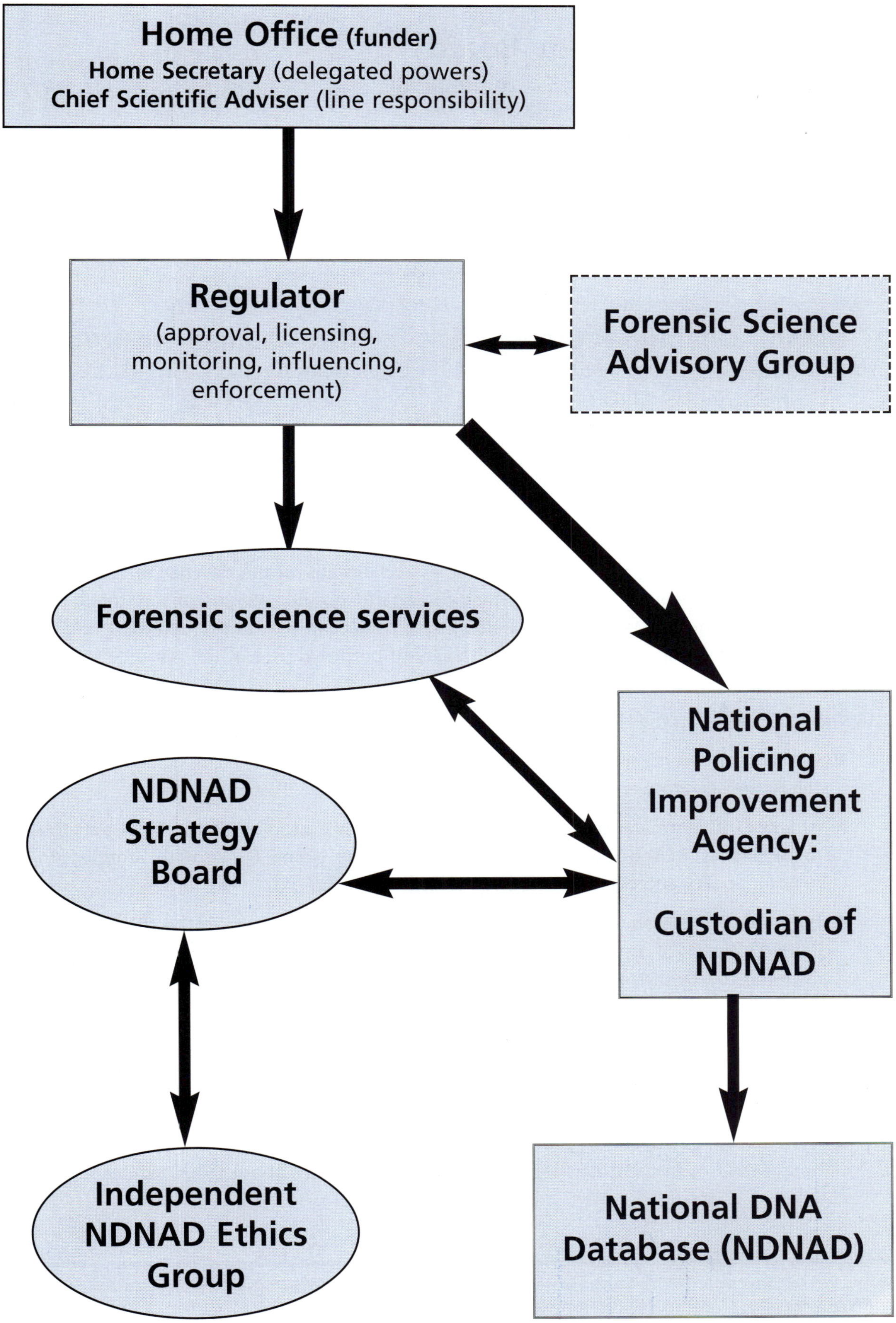

More specifically, the governance arrangement for the NDNAD looks like this:

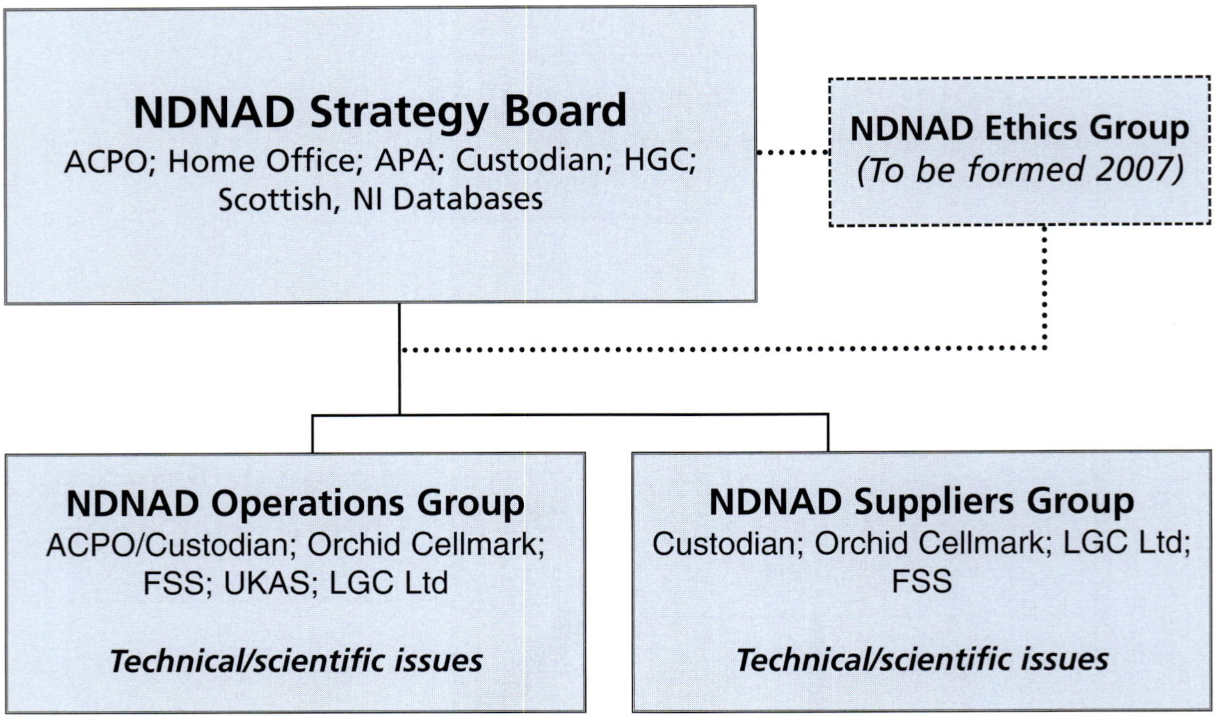

7.17 Other reforming measures that have been reported include: (a) the revision of consent documents for volunteers who provide samples and profiles for the NDNAD; (b) clarification of the provisions to achieve full and informed consent; (c) possible revision of the strict guidelines on removal from the Database (see below) with respect to volunteers; and (d) a role for the NDNAD Ethics Group in assessing the suitability of proposed uses of the resource for research purposes.

7.18 The proposals from the Home Office have been criticised on a number of fronts, including:

- *lack of transparency* – the Regulator will be appointed by, and exercise delegated powers of, the Home Secretary and will be housed within the Home Office;
- *issues of influence and control* – the relocation of the Custodian Unit to NPIA puts the Unit more directly in the realm of policing, leaving the Home Office with arms-length, yet ongoing, policy and overall management responsibilities;
- *questions of independence* – the role of the Regulator in relation to the NDNAD would be limited in terms of assessing its impact on the detection and deterrence of crime and public attitudes towards DNA sampling and profile retention; and
- *concerns about accountability and trust* – lack of an independent relationship from the Home Office and unclear lines of accountability and the criteria on which this will be judged.[18]

7.19 The emerging structure also gives rise to a number of questions as to the respective roles and remits of the Regulator, as well as for existing and new advisory or oversight bodies. A major concern is a lack of detail on the specific tasks and powers of any oversight body or official. Although the Government has responded to specific concerns about the NDNAD and has now

18. See, for example, Liberty (2006) *Liberty's Response to the Home Office Consultation: "Standard Setting and Quality Regulation in Forensic Science"*; and GeneWatch UK (2006) Submission to the Home Office Consultation; and British Academy of Forensic Science (2006) Response to the Home Office Consultation Document.

taken steps in respect of that Database by establishing the Ethics Group, broader issues remain relatively unaddressed: for example those mentioned in Chapter 6 about the extended uses of the NDNAD, the transparency of non-operational research and the retention of information by private DNA analysis providers. At the time of writing, it is unclear what the exact remit and powers of the Ethics Group will be. The public advert for a Chair and members is silent on the issues, while the NDNAD Annual Report for 2005–2006 states that the Strategy Board will have discretion over whether or not to act on any advice offered by the Group.[19] This implies it may have relatively little influence.

7.20 Three main areas of governance require considerably more thought. These are: (1) accountability; (2) ethical oversight; and (3) quality assurance. Examples of good governance in each of these areas already operate elsewhere, and valuable lessons could be learned.

Accountability

7.21 A good model of openness and accountability can be drawn from within the criminal justice system in the form of the Independent Police Complaints Commission (IPCC). The IPCC was established by the Police Reform Act 2002. Its statutory basis lays out very clearly its independence and functions. These include: (a) the handling of complaints made about the conduct of persons serving with the police; (b) securing of public confidence in these matters; and (c) making recommendations or giving advice on possible modifications to these matters as necessary. While the IPCC is funded by the Home Office, its independence is enshrined in robust appointment provisions within the Act. Transparency is facilitated by a duty to report annually to the Secretary of State. These reports are then published.

Ethical oversight

7.22 The world of medical research provides a good example of ethical oversight. UK Biobank is the world's largest longitudinal study into gene–environment interaction. It aims to recruit 500,000 individuals aged 40 to 69, taking their blood and urine samples and base-line health measurements, and having ongoing access to participants' medical records throughout their lives and after death. Participation is voluntary and participants can withdraw at any time. The funders considered the scope and importance of the project required an Ethics and Governance Framework (EGF) which established the parameters within which the project would be conducted.

7.23 The EGF deals with consent, confidentiality, rights of withdrawal, access to the resource and commercialisation. Moreover, the EGF established the Ethics and Governance Council. The Council is an independent body set up following public advertisement and with external assessors on the appointing committee. Its task is to act as a guardian of the EGF, advise on its revision, and monitor and report publicly on UK Biobank's conformity with it. This means that the EGF is not merely a statement of good intentions, nor is it a set of purely abstract principles. It is a working document. The Council meets quarterly and has signed a Memorandum of Understanding with the UK Biobank Board of Directors. Its membership draws from a wide range of professional and lay backgrounds, and members are appointed in accordance with principles of public life.[20] The Council publishes minutes of its meetings, which are sometimes held in public. UK Biobank, for its part, is committed to transparency through publication of its Standard Operating Procedures (SOPs). To perform its task, the Council has full access to all relevant committees and documents of UK Biobank, and can request updates on the progress of the project at any time. The Council does not have the power to veto projects if they fail to

19. 11 March 2007 *The Sunday Times*; National DNA Database (2007) *The National DNA Database Annual Report 2005–2006*, p5.

20. The Seven Principles of Public Life were drawn up by the Nolan Committee and have been endorsed by Parliament. They are: Selflessness; Integrity; Objectivity; Accountability; Openness; Honesty; and Leadership.

conform to the Framework – UK Biobank itself holds the responsibility for ethical stewardship of the resource. If it fails, the Council will report that publicly – and such loss of public trust should vitiate the whole enterprise.

Quality assurance

7.24 It is unclear how far current proposals envisage a quality assurance inspectorate for existing and new service providers within the forensic sciences. There is a need for an independent and trusted body to undertake such a role, perhaps through licensing and regular inspection, and a possible model in this respect is the Human Fertilisation and Embryology Authority (HFEA), which has the primary responsibility for ensuring the highest quality of services in the fertility sector, as well as a custodian role over uses of gametes and embryos. The HFEA was established by statute, with clearly defined authority and powers, including an inspectorate role for fertility clinics and research facilities. Criminal sanctions are imposed for non-compliance with the principal provisions of the legislation, with revocation of licences providing a further sanction against breaches of licence conditions.[21]

7.25 **We recommend the development of a clear ethics and governance framework for the operation of the Ethics Group in order to establish:**

- **its relationship with the NDNAD Strategic Board;**
- **its remit – whether this be to monitor and/or advise or otherwise;**
- **its responsibilities for reporting publicly and handling complaints;**
- **its powers; and**
- **how it is to maintain its independence.**

Further consideration should be given to broader ethical oversight and governance in respect of the umbrella role of the Forensic Science Regulator and other forensic databases, such as IDENT1.

Data protection and human rights

7.26 There is no statutory basis for the operation of the NDNAD or IDENT1 or for their governance. Instead, the development of the law has been piecemeal, leaving uncertainty in places. Notwithstanding this, the NDNAD and IDENT1 are subject to the laws governing human rights and data protection. We have already noted the position in respect of human rights in Chapter 3 (paragraphs 3.29–3.34).

7.27 Both IDENT1 and the NDNAD are governed by European-wide data protection laws and are registered under the Data Protection Act 1998. The law requires that the processing of personal data must comply with eight key principles. These dictate that the data must be processed fairly and lawfully, for specified purposes, respecting subjects' rights. They must be accurate and up to date, and should not be transferred to any country that does not have adequate data protection. Certain exemptions apply when data are processed for the prevention or detection of crime and the administration of justice.[22] In particular, data subjects can be denied their right of access, and the requirement that the data be processed fairly and lawfully does not apply, permitting the police to share data with other agencies. (International transfer is discussed in paragraphs 7.42–7.53.)

7.28 The Police National Computer (PNC) has over 120,000 terminals across the country and holds over seven million records on individuals. Each record will typically include details of arrest,

21. Clinics are regulated through a licensing mechanism so that clinics may only provide services to the public when in possession of a licence, for which a clinic must meet certain criteria. If the clinic cannot meet the criteria, a licence may be withheld or revoked.

22. See Data Protection Act 1998, S. 29.

demographic details, a link to their entry on IDENT1, and whether a biological sample has been taken (and at what point in the process it is), but does not include the fingerprints or DNA profile itself. Thus access to the PNC does not automatically entail access to the bioinformation databases; it will only inform the user that the individual has records on these other databases. IDENT1 is used by all the police forces in England, Wales and Scotland. In addition to 45 fingerprint bureaux in England and Wales, British Transport Police, the Serious Organised Crime Agency (SOCA) and HM Revenue and Customs can access IDENT1. Approximately 1,200 police personnel have direct access to the fingerprint system as well as the Home Office Immigration and Nationality Directorate.

7.29 New ACPO Guidelines on the PNC incorporate a 'step-down model', which restricts access to certain data for non-police users after certain time limits. This permits the police to continue having access to data which non-police agencies should no longer be able to access. Time limits are determined by reference to the age of the subject, the final outcome of the case, the sentence imposed and the category of offence. For example, records for convictions for serious crimes receiving custodial sentences of over six months are not 'stepped down', so details remain available to non-police agencies. Information that relates to events that do not result in a conviction are 'stepped-down' when they are entered onto the PNC, making them unavailable to non-police agencies, although the details remain visible to police when using the PNC. Applications by non-police bodies to access records on the PNC are considered by a Panel chaired by the ACPO lead for Recording and Disclosure of Convictions.[23]

7.30 Access to the NDNAD is currently an arcane procedure because there appears to be no public documentation that sets out a dedicated access policy. The Custodian controls access and it is simply stated that access is restricted to a small number of people for the purposes of the prevention or detection of crime, the investigation of an offence, the conduct of a prosecution or the identification of a deceased person, as laid down in the Police and Criminal Evidence Act 1984 (PACE). The NDNAD Annual Report 2005–2006 states that all requests for access to biological samples or data for research purposes are considered by the NDNAD Strategy Board. The Board takes account of a range of issues, including the legality of the purpose of the request, the requirements of the criminal justice system, data protection laws and the public interest.[24] Advice can be taken from the lay members of the Board (from the Human Genetics Commission) as well as from the Information Commissioner if necessary. It is anticipated that the newly established NDNAD Ethics Group would also have a role to play in access requests, at least those involving research.[25] It is interesting to observe that no equivalent group is envisaged for IDENT1 or other forensic databases. In addition, although it might be argued that this is because they are not concerned with such sensitive data as the NDNAD, the prospect of their future linkage to increase the overall power of their cumulative effect does give rise to concerns about increased risks to privacy. Which body or official will consider applications for linkage or research in the future?

7.31 As stated previously, the private companies storing the biological samples on behalf of police forces regularly access these samples for quality assurance procedures or for re-analysis for match verification purposes. Access to identifying information, so that the DNA provider could be identified, appears to be strictly controlled, and any proposal for access for research purposes would require permission from the Strategy Board. In addition, it has been stated in a ministerial statement to the House of Commons that any extension to the uses to which the NDNAD may be put would be subject to public scrutiny and debate.[26] Sensitivities over potential (ab)use

23. ACPO (2006) *Retention Guidelines for Nominal Records on the Police National Computer.*

24. National DNA Database (2007) *The National DNA Database Annual Report 2005–2006*, p43.

25. Response to our consultation on behalf of the Association of Police Authorities, the Association of Chief Police Officers and the Home Office.

26. Mr Vernon Coaker, Parliamentary Under-Secretary of State for the Home Department, Hansard, 15 November 2006, column 125.

suggest that, for example, searches for information on genetic relations would remain proscribed. Yet access to forensic databases for research purposes remains an under-regulated area, and may remain so while the criteria themselves remain vague (see Chapter 6).

7.32 **In addition to the recommendations made in Chapter 6, we recommend not only that there must be robust procedures for assessing applications for research access to the NDNAD and stored samples, but that there should also be a requirement to articulate publicly the basis upon which applications for any access to data stored on bioinformation databases will be considered and the precise purposes for which access will, and will not, be granted either to police or non-police agencies.**

The importance of independence

The discretion of Chief Constables to remove profiles and samples

7.33 Public trust and confidence will not be maintained if arrangements and procedures are perceived to be partisan or self-serving. A good example of a problem area in this regard is the current provisions for handling requests to remove profiles from the NDNAD or to destroy samples or fingerprints. Individuals are able to request the removal of their individual record(s) from the PNC and linked databases such as IDENT1 and the NDNAD. There is uniform guidance provided by ACPO to Chief Constables regarding the removal of such records. This guidance states that records should only be removed in 'exceptional cases', which may include those where the arrest or sampling was unlawful, or where there was no offence prompting the arrest. The applicants themselves must demonstrate why their case is exceptional.[27]

7.34 Once these guidelines become established, a library of precedents will be maintained on what has previously been considered 'exceptional'. Yet although the guidelines are intended to ensure consistency, there is no substantive guidance on how to determine if a case is exceptional. Decisions therefore risk being arbitrary and potentially unjust. It is not clear, for example, if misconduct or police error could be grounds for removal, such as in the case of mistaken identity and arrest involving a juvenile who could not then have his profile erased despite the error.[28] There is no apparent appeal process, although it is assumed that a judicial review of a decision by a Chief Officer would be possible.

7.35 This approach is to be contrasted with the position in Germany where authorities must show a likelihood that someone will (re)offend with a recordable offence before retention of samples is possible (see Box. 4.3). Thus, in Germany and indeed Scotland, the state must justify retention, whereas in England and Wales the burden falls on the individual to show why retention should not be permanent (see Chapter 4).

7.36 We have earlier recommended that while indefinite retention of fingerprints and DNA profiles is justified from those convicted of a recordable offence (paragraph 4.54), subject samples and the resulting profiles of those not charged or convicted should be destroyed except in the case of serious violent and sexual offenders – where Chief Constables may apply to a court for retention for two years (paragraph 4.55). We have also suggested a presumption in favour of the removal of records of minors.

27. *Exceptional Case Procedures for Removal DNA, Fingerprints and PNC Records*, April 2006, available at: www.acpo.police.uk/policies.asp, accessed on: 11 July 2007. See also, *ACPO Retention Guidelines for Nominal Records on the Police National Computer*, Appendix 2, 2006: www.homeoffice.gov.uk/documents/Bichard_Step_Model_Retention.pdf?view=Binary, accessed on: 11 July 2007.

28. Taylor N and Roberts A (2006) Genes on record: one size fits all? *New Law Journal* **156:** 1354; 9 January 2006 *Daily Telegraph*.

7.37 **At present, the 'exceptional circumstances' criteria for removal of records from the NDNAD and other databases are too restrictive, and the Chief Constable's discretion too wide. If the current system remains and records are not automatically removed for those not convicted, in accordance with our earlier recommendations (paragraphs 4.53–4.55 and 4.72), we recommend that:**

- **There should be public guidelines explaining how to apply to have records removed from police databases, and the grounds on which removal can be required.**
- **The police should be required to justify the need for retention in response to a request for removal of an individual (with a strong presumption in favour of removal in the case of minors, see paragraph 4.72).**
- **An independent body, along the lines of an administrative tribunal, should oversee requests from individuals to have their profiles removed from bioinformation databases. The tribunal would have to balance the rights of the individual against such factors as the seriousness of the offence, previous arrests, the outcome of the arrest, the likelihood of this individual re-offending, the danger to the public and any other special circumstances.**

The integration of forensic databases: the emerging challenge of linkage

7.38 Moves to integrate forensic bioinformation databases with each other and with other police and criminal records databases have recently become a priority.[29] However, any integration must retain the integrity of the individual databases, and ensure that safeguards are in place to protect the data from misuse. The possible 'sharing' or cross-referencing of forensic databases, as well as the potential for forensic use of non-forensic databases or the non-forensic use of forensic databases, are a possible further cause for concern. Many of our respondents and those who gave oral evidence pointed to the risks associated both with increased linkage and the cross-over between civil 'security' and criminal justice databases. There are also fears that as databases containing sensitive personal data proliferate (including databases for medical research such as UK Biobank and even databases for the fingerprints of schoolchildren, see paragraph 4.6), police access under some circumstances may be harder to resist in the future.[30]

7.39 The House of Commons Science and Technology Committee has pointed to the potential of linkage to other (forensic) databases and recommended that the police and the Home Office pay adequate attention to custodian and access arrangements as well as data sharing mechanisms.[31] We have offered the example of IDENT1 as a platform that currently exists and which is ideally suited to facilitate record linkage across an entire range of forensic databases in the future.

7.40 While the variety of forensic biometric databases are not currently linked in any sophisticated fashion, it is a stated aim for databases to be 'inter-operable' in the near future.[32] The ethical implications of such databases could then be 'multiplied' by linking with other databases, most particularly with respect to concerns about privacy. Those concerns may be further compounded if linkage is envisaged between databases across different countries, as we discuss in the next section.

---

29. See, for example, the Bichard Inquiry into the Soham murders, whose recommendations included a national information technology system, adequate investment in the Police National Computer and a new code of practice on information management, see http://www.bichardinquiry.org.uk, accessed on: 16 July 2007.
30. Note, however, both UK Biobank and its sister project, Generation Scotland, have indicated that they would vigorously resist any attempt by police for access to their genetic resources.
31. House of Commons Science and Technology Select Committee (2005) *Forensic Science on Trial*, paragraphs 90–9.
32. See (most recently) *PITO Business Plan 2006/07*.

The challenges of international exchange

7.41 Countries throughout the European Union and beyond are expanding their bioinformation databases,[33] and demands are increasingly being made for data to be shared among international law enforcement agencies. The importance of cooperation over DNA technologies in particular is recognised by domestic and international law enforcement agencies.[34] The European Commission has expressed a desire that there be direct, online access to DNA databases across Europe.[35] However, current barriers to safe and efficient sharing include:

- disparate legal regimes on the protection of DNA and genetic data, albeit that the Data Protection Directive is a Europe-wide instrument;
- disparate collection regimes for the taking and retention of DNA: the United Kingdom has by far the most permissive regime in Europe with a DNA database larger than the sum of all others in the Union;
- absence of legal agreements on sharing and exchange of data (see. Prüm Treaty, paragraph 7.50);
- non-standardisation of databases and formats across countries;
- lack of compatible technical systems to ease sharing and ensure inter-operability;
- need for all countries to meet minimum agreed standards on information held on databases; and
- paucity of formal procedures to facilitate cross-border investigation and data sharing.

7.42 **We recommend, on the basis of standard European data protection principles, a minimum set of safeguarding requirements to consider before allowing access to bioinformation databases to international law enforcement agencies, which would be:**

- **to ensure there is a sufficient level of data protection in all authorities/agencies that would receive information;**
- **to subject each request to adequate scrutiny as to merit and reasonableness and on a transparent basis;**
- **to agree the criteria for sharing data, for example only for the investigation of serious crimes or in special circumstances; and**
- **to share only as much information as is necessary to meet the request and only to those authorities or agencies which 'need to know'.**

7.43 European Technical Standards fall within the auspices of the European Network of Forensic Science Institutes (ENFSI), which has agreed processes to facilitate exchange of forensic data. The ENFSI DNA Working Group has agreed a standard common seven markers as a minimum DNA profile. In practice, most countries, including the United Kingdom, rely on standards that require more markers (SGM+ uses ten markers). This could raise issues about variation across Europe and could increase the error rate. A common safeguard, however, is that a match alone cannot lead to prosecution in the absence of further evidence (see Chapter 5).

7.44 Exchanges of data are currently made on a case-by-case basis, with no internationally agreed

33. See European Network of Forensic Science Institutes DNA Working Group (2006) *Report on ENFSI Member Countries' DNA Database Legislation Survey.*

34. Parliamentary Office of Science and Technology (2006) PostNote *The National DNA Database*, Number 258, p3.

35. As an alternative to direct access, requests for data can be handled internally by a governance body and the enquirer can be provided with data that are suitably protected, e.g. through anonymisation. Such a model operates within the UK health services for certain kinds of health research. Such requests are scrutinised by independent dedicated bodies, namely the Patient Information Advisory Group in England and Wales and the Privacy Advisory Committee in Scotland.

framework for sharing data.[36] Various initiatives are underway to facilitate exchanges while maintaining quality standards and adequate levels of protection for individual rights. This is important because, as noted in paragraph 7.27, not all countries have the same safeguards in place for the protection of data. Because the integrity of forensic databases is vital to ensuring public trust and confidence, greater sharing of sensitive personal data across national borders may be problematic. The process of exchanging DNA profiles entails 'personal' information leaving the jurisdiction in which it was obtained, with little by way of assurance that it will not be subjected to unauthorised storage and use. There is no oversight body to monitor the international exchange of DNA profiles, nor any organisation that could make enquiries (and pursue complaints) on behalf of individuals whose data have been misused. Concerns over such a lack of oversight are heightened by recent proposals for a centralised database of fingerprints across the European Union, with an attendant obligation on each Member State to transfer details held by national police forces to a central authority.[37]

7.45 Interpol established a DNA database in June 2003, for the use of member countries to compare selected DNA profiles they have collected with those collected by other member countries. This database became operational at the end of 2005. It is directly accessible for single or multiple requests by 33 member countries who may contribute to the database. Interpol has protocols for international exchange of data on a case-by-case basis, with DNA profiles able to be stored and searched across international borders using the Interpol Standard Set Of Loci (ISSOL). There have been two significant exchanges of DNA information in the past three years, with the United Kingdom sending unsolved crime scene profiles overseas in an effort to produce a match with a subject profile held on a DNA database in another country. In October 2004, 1,687 DNA crime scene profiles from undetected sexual offences in the UK were submitted to the Interpol DNA database (through the UK National Central Bureau for Interpol (NCB)). In February 2006, 10,763 DNA crime scene profiles from unsolved serious crimes committed in the UK were sent to the Netherlands for checking against the Netherlands DNA database.[38]

7.46 An Interpol DNA Charter has been developed to provide a suitable regulatory framework. Oversight is provided by a DNA Monitoring Expert Group (MEG) which comprises leading DNA experts from member countries. There is a proposal to allow individual countries to retain DNA within their borders but to allow searches by other countries (the UK's preferred option). The UK NCB undertakes risk assessments of all requests for searches to be undertaken against the NDNAD from overseas law enforcement agencies. It is not known on what basis this is done, although searching has been carried out through the NDNAD Custodian. The number of overseas requests that have been granted to exchange DNA information from the UK is small: 121 subject profiles from the NDNAD were provided to the UK NCB between August 2004 and May 2006, while 398 NDNAD search results (from running unsolved crime scene samples from overseas against the UK NDNAD to see if any subject profiles produced a match) were provided to the UK NCB in response to overseas requests in the years 2004/5 and 2005/6.[39] Interpol has recently launched a DNA Gateway, to which the UK is a signatory, and by which DNA profiles can be compared online for matches. Profiles are held anonymously.[40] The Interpol database is not used for familial searching.

7.47 Whilst DNA profiles are sent outside the United Kingdom under exemptions in the Data Protection Act 1998, there has been no systematic Government consideration of this specific

---

36. Since 2004 there have been 519 requests from foreign countries from information from the NDNAD; Joan Ryan MP, 5 June 2006, Hansard, column 278W.

37. Charter D (2007) Central fingerprint database plan draws fire from all over EU *The Times*, 16 March.

38. Andy Burnham MP, Hansard, 18 April 2006, column 446W.

39. Joint response to our consultation on behalf of the Association of Police Authorities, the Association of Chief Police Officers and the Home Office.

40. National DNA Database (2007) *The National DNA Database Annual Report 2005–2006*, p45.

issue. Nor are there guidelines for the handling and exchange of DNA profiles other than those set out in the general provisions of Title VI of the Treaty on European Union (which provides for a 'bridge' between member countries to achieve the objectives of the Union, and sets out 'common interests' such as justice and home affairs, which members agree to cooperate upon), and in Title IV of the Europol Convention (which outlines parameters for the storage and use of personal information).

7.48 The European Union's ambitions for strengthening freedom, security and justice include an aspiration for borderless flows of information from 1 January 2008. The European Council Framework Decision of 2005 has sought to promote this objective while ensuring the protection of personal data exchanged between police and judicial bodies of Member States.[41] Conditions to be observed include: protecting sources, maintaining confidentiality, achieving common standards for access as well as common technical standards for sampling and profiling, and uniform protection of individuals from abuse. This Framework Decision would require that personal data used by competent authorities must be:

- processed fairly and lawfully;
- collected for specified, explicit and legitimate purposes;
- adequate, relevant and not excessive;
- accurate and, where necessary, kept up to date; and
- kept in a form that permits identification of data subjects for no longer than is necessary.

7.49 The Framework Decision concerns information exchange of six kinds of data, including DNA and fingerprints, and introduces direct (online) access to databases. Europol would have same rights of access. The primary obligation is to forward information directly to a requesting party, save in certain specified circumstances, for example, to protect individuals, or to protect confidentiality or other fundamental freedoms.

7.50 The Prüm Treaty (2005) is an existing cooperation agreement of eleven Member States[42] for exchange of information and has been offered as a model for the entire European Union. It provides for:

- direct access to foreign databases on a hit/no hit basis;
- automated comparison of profiles of untraceable people by mutual consent (again on a hit/no hit basis); and
- collection of biological samples and supply of DNA profiles.

7.51 The direct access provisions would not apply until the data protection elements of the Treaty have been adopted into national laws. The Prüm Working Party has also recommended that new laws would be required in signatory countries to allow familial searching under the Treaty. Importantly, the 2007 German Presidency proposed that the Treaty be transposed into EU law, which would then require it to be implemented into the laws of all 27 Member States. Any such initiative would, however, require unanimity to be adopted, and this may take several years with no guarantee of success.

7.52 These initiatives were recently considered by the House of Lords European Union Committee which expressed considerable disquiet about the way in which a multilateral treaty like Prüm had made its way onto the EU legislative agenda.[43] Although there are constitutional and

41. Proposal for a Council framework decision on the protection of personal data processed in the framework of police and judicial cooperation in criminal matters, *Official Journal* L 069,16/03/2005 P. 0067–0071, available at: http://ec.europa.eu/justice_home/doc_centre/privacy/law/index_en.htm, accessed on: 6 July 2007. Member States had to take necessary measures to comply with the Decision by 16 March 2007.

42. Austria, Belgium, France, Germany, Luxembourg, the Netherlands, Spain, Finland, Italy, Portugal and Slovenia.

43. House of Lords, European Union Committee (2007) *Prüm: An Effective Weapon Against Terrorism and Crime?* HL Paper 90.

procedural issues at stake, these are not the concern of this Report. Rather, the value of the House of Lords report lies in its identification of key matters which must be addressed before there is any progress towards European harmonisation, whether this be by means of the Commission's Decision Framework[44] or a modified version of the Prüm Treaty.[45] Two recommendations of the EU Committee are directly pertinent to our conclusions and we endorse them here as recommendations. **The threshold for holding DNA profiles on a forensic database is far lower in the United Kingdom than in any other Member State of the EU, and the proportion of the population included on the UK DNA Database is correspondingly far higher than in other EU countries. The Government should as a matter of urgency examine the implications of DNA exchanges for those on the United Kingdom NDNAD. The Government should insist on the inclusion in the Prüm Treaty of provisions to ensure that its operation is properly monitored. At the very least, the following is required:**

- **an obligation on national agencies to produce annual reports, including statistics, on the use of their powers under the Treaty; and**
- **an obligation on the European Commission to produce an overall evaluation of the operation of the Treaty, for submission to the European Council, the European Parliament and national parliaments, to see whether it needs amendment.**[46]

Despite a Europe-wide data protection regime which has existed since the adoption of the Data Protection Directive in 1995, specific matters as they relate to 'police and judicial cooperation in criminal matters' – the so-called 'third pillar' of the EU – have not been addressed in any depth. The Government should seize the opportunity to stipulate that they will agree to the Prüm Treaty only if other Member States simultaneously agree to a Framework Decision setting high standards for the protection of data across the third pillar.[47]

7.53 In summary, privacy-related issues concerning the use and transfer of DNA and other data for inter-jurisdictional criminal matters must be considered and agreed *in parallel* with arrangements for availability, exchange and linkage.

The future in the United Kingdom

7.54 The current regulatory structure is not on a statutory footing and the legislative framework surrounding the forensic use of bioinformation is piecemeal and patchy. The regulatory architecture of forensic services is also currently in a state of flux in the United Kingdom. While different areas of the industry might require specific attention, such as the NDNAD, there is a need to think more holistically and prospectively about the future possibilities and challenges that might come with increased access to, and sharing of data, across forensic databases. An essential aspect of all governance arrangements must be a commitment to transparency and openness both as regards standard operating procedures (SOPs) and decision-making processes. This is in addition to the requirement that those procedures and processes be justifiable in the first place. Another crucial feature of the regulatory structure is the role of an independent oversight body or official.

44. The House of Lords Committee opines that the Commission proposal risks becoming redundant, there being no further negotiations at the time of writing, see paragraph 18.

45. The House of Lords Committee urges the UK Government to take advantage of the need for unanimity to adopt Prüm at the European level in order to negotiate a better set of provisions than are currently available, Chapter 4 *What Should the United Kingdom Be Doing?*

46. *Ibid.*, paragraph 80.

47. *Ibid.*, paragraph 91. The European Union takes decisions in three separate 'domains' (policy areas), also known as the 'three pillars' of the EU. The first pillar is the 'Community domain', covering most of the common policies, where decisions are taken by the 'Community method' – involving the Commission, Parliament and the Council. The second pillar is the common foreign and security policy, where decisions are taken by the Council alone. The third pillar is 'police and judicial cooperation in criminal matters', where again the Council alone takes the decisions.

7.55 **We recommend that there should be a statutory basis for the regulation of forensic databases and retained biological samples. A regulatory framework should be established with a clear statement of purpose and specific powers of oversight delegated to an appropriate independent body or official. This should include oversight of research and other access requests, for example for further testing of samples or familial searching and inferring ethnicity. We are pleased to see the establishment of an Ethics Group by the Home Office, with a remit to oversee the running and uses of the NDNAD, but its specific functions and powers must be more clearly, and publicly, articulated. Moreover, we consider that a longer-term view is required that considers the future possibilities and challenges that may come with increased access and linkage involving a range of forensic databases.**

7.56 Throughout this Report we have drawn attention to the difficulty in assessing the impact of increasing police powers because of the poor quality or absence of official statistics (or conflicting statistics). Moreover, on many vital issues such as requests to conduct research on databases and/or samples or general access provisions to the NDNAD, there is an absence of protocols or guidance open to public scrutiny.

7.57 **We recommend a far greater commitment to openness and transparency and a greater availability of documents to public scrutiny. Where public access is denied for reasons of security and the administration of justice, this should be fully explained and justified. Efforts to improve the generation of data and statistics are welcomed, as are apparent efforts to increase the publication of data. These moves are still in their early stages, and their continuation is strongly supported.**

Appendices

Appendix 1: Method of working

In early 2006, the Council held a workshop to discuss the issues that arise from the forensic use of bioinformation. It subsequently decided to establish a Working Group on the subject. The Working Group met four times between September 2006 and May 2007, and also held several fact-finding meetings, detailed below. The Working Group is very grateful to all those who gave their time and expert advice and contributed greatly to this Report.

Fact-finding meetings[1]

22 January 2007

Ms Karen Squibb-Williams, Crown Prosecution Service

Mr Robert Green, Police Standards Unit

Mr Mike McMullen, ACPO Fingerprint/ DNA Retention Programme

16 February 2007

Visit to Forensic Science Service Headquarters, Birmingham

12 March 2007

Dr Ric Treble, LGC Forensics

Mr David Charlton, Sussex Police Fingerprints Expert

16 March 2007

Simon Moore and Geoff Whitaker, Police Information Technology Organisation (PITO)

Matthew Greenhalgh and David Hartshorne, Orchid Cellmark (private company providing DNA analysis)

1. Institutional affiliations at the time of the meeting are listed.

Appendix 2: Wider consultation

A consultation was held between November 2006 and January 2007. A consultation paper prepared by the Working Group contained background information and questions for respondents to answer if they wished. The document was disseminated to individuals and organisations relevant to the field and it was also available online. Approximately 135 responses to the consultation were received; 76 per cent from individuals and 24 per cent from organisations.

The Working Group and the Council are grateful for such a diverse range of responses and found them to be insightful and useful. The questions, a summary of the responses and the list of respondents are provided in this Appendix. The views that have been included in this summary were selected either to display the range of different comments or to highlight particularly interesting perspectives. The summary is not intended to form a quantitative survey. Many respondents agreed to make their submissions available publicly and these can be found on the Council's website.

Questions in the consultation paper

1. The interpretation of bioinformation

In your view, is the SGM Plus® system, which uses ten STR markers, sufficiently reliable for use in ascertaining the identity of suspects in criminal investigations and/or criminal trials?

2. Sampling powers

a. From whom should the police be able to take fingerprints and biological samples? At what stages in criminal investigations and for what purposes? Should the police be able to request further information from DNA analysts, such as physical characteristics or ethnic inferences?

b. Should police expenditure on bioinformation collection and analysis be given priority over other budgetary demands?

c. Do you consider the current criteria for the collection of bioinformation to be proportionate to the aims of preventing, investigating, detecting and prosecuting criminal offences? In particular: is the retention of bioinformation from those who are not convicted of an offence proportionate to the needs of law enforcement?

d. Is it acceptable for bioinformation to be taken from minors and for their DNA profiles to be put on the National DNA Database (NDNAD)?

3. The management of the NDNAD

a. Is it proportionate for bioinformation from i) suspects and ii) volunteers to be kept on forensic databases indefinitely? Should criminal justice and elimination samples also be kept indefinitely? How should the discretion of Chief Constables to remove profiles and samples from the NDNAD be exercised and overseen?

b. Is the ethical oversight of the NDNAD adequate? What, if any, research on NDNAD profiles or samples should be permitted? Who should be involved in the oversight of such databases and granting permission to use forensic DNA profiles or samples for research?

c. Who should have access to information on the NDNAD and IDENT1 databases and how should bioinformation be protected from unauthorised uses and users? Should forensic databases ever be made available for non-criminal investigations, such as parental searches, or the identification of missing or deceased persons?

d. What issues are raised by the transfer of bioinformation between agencies and countries? How should such transfers be facilitated and what safeguards should be in place for the storage and use of transferred data?

4. Ethical issues

a. Is the use of DNA profiles in 'familial searching' inquiries proportionate to the needs of criminal investigations? Do you consider the use of familial searching may be an unwarranted invasion of family privacy?

b. Certain groups, such as ethnic minorities and young males, are disproportionately represented on forensic databases. Is this potential for bias within these databases acceptable?

c. Is it acceptable that volunteers (such as victims, witnesses, mass screen volunteers) also have their profiles retained on the NDNAD? Should consent be irrevocable for individuals who agree initially to the retention of samples voluntarily given to the police? Are the provisions for obtaining consent appropriate? Should volunteers be able to withdraw their consent at a later stage?

d. Would the collection of DNA from everyone at birth be more equitable than collecting samples from only those who come into contact with the criminal justice system? Would the establishment of such a population-wide forensic database be proportionate to the needs of law enforcement? What are the arguments for and against an extension of the database?

5. The evidential value of bioinformation

a. What should be done to ensure that police, legal professionals, witnesses and jury members have sufficient understanding of any forensic bioinformation relevant to their participation in the criminal justice system?

b. How much other evidence should be required before a defendant can be convicted in a case with a declared DNA match? Should a DNA match ever be taken to be sufficient to prove guilt in the absence of other evidence?

6. Other issues

a. Are there any other issues, within our terms of reference, which we should consider?

Summary of responses

1. The interpretation of bioinformation: SGM+ system

Opinion was divided over whether the SGM+ system was or was not sufficiently reliable. One respondent thought the issue should be regularly reviewed. The joint response from the Association of Police Authorities, the Association of Chief Police Officers and the Home Office stated that these organisations were confident that the current profiling system would not lead to any miscarriages of justice. It confirmed that, when matches were made from crime scenes to profiles that had been recorded on the NDNAD using the former SGM system, associated biological samples would be "routinely reanalysed using SGM+". However, the organisations noted that, as the NDNAD continued to increase in size and there was greater interchange of information with other national DNA databases, there would be a need in the future to enhance the discriminating power of the profiling system. Several potential technologies that might be used for this purpose were suggested. A different problem was identified by another respondent who thought that any technology, no matter how reliable, could be misused. The possibility of unintentional human error was also raised, a point that should be recognised when evidence involving DNA was presented in a court of law.

2. Sampling powers

When should the police be able to take bioinformation?

There was quite considerable support from respondents for the police being able to take bioinformation during the investigation of a case as and when they felt appropriate, and, further, to be able to request any information from DNA analysts that would assist in the detection of a crime. Others were more hesitant, and thought that further information should be requested only when it became "necessary". Some respondents wished to see as little use of DNA evidence as possible and thought that it should only be used when a suspect had already been implicated as a result of other evidence or when guilt had been proven. Others thought that samples should only be taken when they would assist the investigation of the offence (the group JUSTICE).

Expenditure on bioinformation collection and analysis

Only a minority of respondents to this question thought that expenditure on bioinformation collection and analysis should be given budgetary priority over other demands. Some specified that this should occur only for techniques that would be cost-effective in reducing crime. One respondent (a police officer) thought that budgetary decisions were a matter for individual Chief Constables.

Quite a number of respondents believed that police expenditure on bioinformation collection and analysis should not be given priority over other budgetary demands, believing that the NDNAD was not making a significant contribution to increasing the number of convictions for serious crimes. Other priorities on which the authorities should direct funding were suggested including community policing and more traditional methods of detection. One respondent felt that "the police should not be wasting money collecting the bioinformation of innocents" (Phil Booth) and this sentiment was mirrored in several other submissions.

Proportionality

The current criteria for the collection of bioinformation (see Chapter 4) were accepted by several respondents as proportionate for its use in the detection of crime. However, there was quite widespread concern among respondents that politicians had decided that bioinformation should be retained from those who were not convicted, which was, in their view, disproportionate. One police officer was of the opinion that, if charged, a person should have their DNA profile retained on the Database, since perpetrators were not always successfully convicted. His view was that it was practical to take DNA at the arrest stage (unless the police officer involved thought this to be disproportionate) and had other advantages such as allowing police officers to engage with suspects outside of the formal interview process. However, this respondent and many others thought that it was inappropriate to retain the DNA profiles and samples of people who were not charged or who had provided samples for elimination purposes. Some respondents commented that Members of Parliament may not have represented their constituents' views when they voted in favour of the retention of profiles and samples from people who had not been convicted. A number were concerned that expansion of the Database could result in an erosion of the assumption of 'innocent until proven guilty'. A selection of their reactions is included below:

"... the collection of bioinformation has gone much too far."

Anon

"Retaining innocent people's DNA data in a database and then later trawling through it for suspects is dangerous in the light of false positive matches."

Anon

"... in some cases detection of crime is secondary to building the database".

Paul Higgins

Support was strong for retaining the profiles of people who had been convicted of an offence, with respondents citing the high prevalence of re-offending. Some respondents proposed that people convicted of lesser crimes should have their records removed after a period of time. Conversely, a few respondents thought the solution could be to establish a programme of recording every citizen's bioinformation. Reasons given included:

"The retention of bioinformation is essential (as is further development of the database) to the future wellbeing of society as it allows for the rapid elimination of [...] persons from future enquiries ..."

Mike Mills

"... our rights as individuals are over-ridden by our duty to help the Police solve crimes, to the benefit of everyone."

Sarah Smith

Inclusion of the profiles of minors on the NDNAD

Generally respondents who supported the introduction of a population-wide DNA database thought that it was acceptable for bioinformation of minors to be included on the NDNAD. Some thought parental consent should be a requirement whereas others thought that the profiles and samples of minors should only be used for pursuing an investigation, but not retained. However, a number of respondents were strongly against retaining the DNA profiles and samples of minors, especially of young children. One correspondent thought that the profile of a minor should be retained on the Database only for a period of time proportionate to the crime for which the person was convicted. Another believed that not retaining on the NDNAD the profiles of minors involved in petty crime would give them "the right and freedom to learn from their mistakes".

3. The management of the NDNAD

Retention of bioinformation

Many respondents were completely opposed to the retention without consent of profiles and samples from suspects not subsequently convicted of a crime and, particularly, from volunteers, believing that it was disproportionate to any benefit. Some thought that it was unfair that innocent people were treated in the same way as known criminals in this regard whereas several considered that the public did not trust the government not to abuse a national database. Others had concerns that data could be sold or otherwise passed on. Some people judged it improper for the state to retain information about its citizens when not strictly necessary.

For convicted criminals, there was little disagreement that their DNA profiles should be retained on the NDNAD, although quite a number of correspondents contributed proposals for how they thought the retention of profiles and samples could be better managed: for example, only the profiles of people convicted of very serious crimes should be retained on the NDNAD; a person's DNA profile (and sample) could be retained on the Database for a time proportionate to the crime committed; or, there should be a set period of time after which a DNA profile (and sample) would be removed if no re-offending had occurred (with certain exceptions for particularly serious offences or if a judge had specifically approved a request for retention). It was suggested that this measure would bring the situation into line with the Rehabilitation of Offenders Act.[1]

There was quite considerable support for more standardised rules rather than allowing the decision to remove profiles from the NDNAD to rest within the discretion of Chief Constables, especially in relation to decisions about innocent people and minors. Chief Constables "could not be expected to do other than to prefer retention" (*David Proctor*). One suggestion was that this process could be managed and overseen by an independent watchdog.

Those who thought that it was proportionate to retain bioinformation from suspects and volunteers were frequently those who thought that the NDNAD should be extended to the whole population, for example "... the information should be supplied voluntarily as a way of life in the UK" (*Dana Moore*). These respondents thought that having their DNA stored was a very small price to pay to help prevent and detect crime.

Ethical oversight and research uses of the NDNAD

A number of respondents suggested that ethical oversight of the NDNAD was inadequate and currently performed inappropriately by people with a vested interest in its functioning. Many suggested that responsibility for ethical oversight should be transferred to an independent body, acting in the interests of the public. Membership might include, for example, legal and technical experts, religious leaders, representatives of organisations that campaign for human rights and civil liberties, and lay people. One correspondent thought that oversight would best be carried out by a civil liberties group.

As regards the research that should be permitted using NDNAD profiles and biological samples, there was some support for allowing access to data only for statistical, non-identifying research. Other respondents suggested that profiles and samples should only be used for other purposes beyond forensics if the people from whom they had been taken had given their consent and were allowed to withdraw their consent in future. Some respondents, however, thought the NDNAD and the corresponding samples should not be treated as a database for research and any use of it for that purpose would constitute non-consensual research and as such should be banned. The concern was voiced that as more people or organisations were given access to the information, the less easy it would be to ensure privacy.

Access to forensic databases

There was strong support for limiting access to forensic databases to police activities and for permission to search the databases only to be granted to trained members of specified police and government agencies. Some respondents proposed that an overseeing body should be given the responsibility of granting warrants to access forensic bioinformation when requested by non-criminal investigators.

Many people held the view that it was inappropriate for paternity investigations to make use of information gathered for forensic use. There was some acceptance for the use of bioinformation collected by the police to be permitted for the identification of deceased persons, although one person thought this should not be allowed because it might be assumed, perhaps wrongly, that the person had been involved in criminal activity.

Transfer of bioinformation

There were mixed views on whether bioinformation should be transferred out of the United Kingdom. Some respondents thought that it would open opportunities for tampering and that

---

[1] The Rehabilitation of Offenders Act 1974 allows for some more minor offences to become 'spent' if the individual does not re-offend during a rehabilitation period. This means that a convicted person does not have to declare the offence (in most circumstances) after this time.

there could be no assurance that use would be appropriately controlled. If supported, it was generally with the qualification that international use should be confined to solving international crimes and terrorism. Other respondents wished to see guarantees that recipient countries had equally strict data protection legislation. Even many of those who were in favour of a DNA database that included everybody in the UK thought that proper controls would be needed when transferring information from such a database abroad.

A couple of respondents suggested that if use of the NDNAD was requested by other agencies or by an agency in a different country, then the requesting agency should submit their request to the NDNAD. The holders of the data in the United Kingdom should then carry out the request (i.e. searches or further analysis of samples) and then report back to the requesting agency, rather than the requesting agency being sent actual data or samples.

One respondent was in favour of more easily available information and had concerns that overregulation could hinder the effective use of data in the public interest. There was support from another respondent for a worldwide DNA database.

4. Ethical issues

'Familial searching'

Many respondents, including somebody who wished to see the NDNAD extended to all citizens, thought that use of the NDNAD for 'familial searching' (see Chapter 6) was a disproportionate breach of privacy compared with any benefits that might be gained. Others thought that familial searching should only be allowed for the most serious of crimes. A number of respondents, however, weighed potential benefits as greater than concerns about privacy, especially if familial searching was confined to the investigation of serious crimes. The Forensic Science Society, for example, thought that the concern about invading family privacy could be overcome if the information found as a result of familial searching was "treated for intelligence purposes only and as sensitive information with adequate consideration before the information is disclosed to a potential family member identified." It was noted by Professor A P Dawid that the discriminatory power of DNA profiling was generally much weaker for familial searches than it was for direct matching of crime scene samples and suspects.

Disproportionate representation of certain groups on the NDNAD

Several respondents found the potential for bias due to over-representation of certain groups on the NDNAD to be unacceptable. A few people suggested that the establishment of a DNA database that included everyone would overcome imbalances of representation on the NDNAD. Several others thought that the risk of bias would be reduced if people who were not convicted were removed. However, it was quite widely perceived among respondents that the over-representation of some groups on the Database was 'inevitable'. Reasons given were, for example, that young males committed more crimes on average than other groups and therefore this 'group' would be highly prevalent on the NDNAD.

Retention of samples from volunteers

Many of those who wished to see the DNA of everybody in the United Kingdom included on a national forensic database did not generally find it problematic that the profiles and samples of volunteers and witnesses (with irrevocable consent) were currently retained. However, many more respondents considered this situation unacceptable and, even, in the words of one correspondent, 'outrageous'. A commonly expressed view was that volunteers should be entitled to withdraw their consent to the retention of their DNA profile and sample at any future point, since their circumstances and beliefs might change.

Many respondents proposed that, unless volunteers had explicitly stated that they did not want their profile removed, it should be deleted once they had been eliminated from the enquiry. If a case remained unsolved, profiles from volunteers should be removed after a set period of time.

Profiling at birth

Several respondents thought that universal DNA profiling at birth for entry on a forensic database would be beneficial and proportionate, believing that it would lead to a reduction in crime and an increase in detection rates. These respondents thought that only criminals would have cause for fear, and law-abiding citizens should not have any reason to be concerned by the expansion of the NDNAD. One respondent considered that everybody should be regarded as a potential suspect in a police investigation until eliminated. He equated an innocent person's DNA being found at a crime scene, as analogous to being wrongly identified by a witness (i.e. the identification of a suspect was on its own, insufficient evidence of guilt). A small number of respondents proposed that all persons entering the United Kingdom should have a biological sample taken at the point of entry.

However, many respondents were strongly against the idea of profiling at birth, citing reasons of violation of personal freedom and civil rights. For example, it was thought that it would constitute an "… unwarranted invasion of privacy" (*Mr Frank Everett*). One respondent was particularly concerned that such a system would mean taking DNA from people "who are in their most vulnerable position – a child" (*Anon*). It was suggested that many people felt that their DNA was personal, private information and that having such a database would turn all citizens into suspects. One respondent stated that he would consider emigrating rather than be subject to such a system. Perceived dangers included miscarriages of justice, denial of services to people with a particular genetic composition, discrimination and revealing of non-paternity. There was also a concern about 'mission creep'; i.e. if other agencies interested in using genetic data, for example to establish paternity, found that future governments were sympathetic to requests for access to a comprehensive national database.

A small number of respondents suggested that holding the genetic profiles of all citizens on a database would be more equitable than the present system but that it would not be proportionate to the needs of detecting crime. It was suggested by a respondent that even if more equitable, profiling at birth would be difficult to impose on people and that therefore the current arrangements were adequate and served the public well.

A few respondents believed that political despots in the past would have been even more dangerous if they had had access to the level of information that would be generated by profiling at birth. There were fears that, if the United Kingdom government were to become malign, there could be unacceptable consequences for innocent people arising from the availability of a database that contained their bioinformation.

5. The evidential value of bioinformation

Understanding of forensic bioinformation by people involved in the criminal justice system

A common view among respondents was that forensic techniques were not well understood, and that juries and the public more widely should be educated in this subject. We were told that courts can think it unnecessary for a statistical expert to attend court hearings to explain the interpretation of statistical evidence relating to match probabilities, the subtleties and complexities of which can be less than straightforward. One respondent commented that the police service itself lacked a good understanding of the value of DNA evidence:

"Police Officers are too easily encouraged to jump to the view that DNA is the answer to all their prayers and to overvalue the evidence."

Anon

Training juries in the significance of DNA evidence was suggested as important. For example, an impartial presentation could be made to juries before trials. This might highlight the fallibility of relying too heavily on forensic bioinformation, the nature of the information available and its associated level of accuracy.

Weight of DNA evidence

It was noted that there was a need to consider the possible ways in which evidence might have come to be at the scene of a crime, and whether DNA could be present accidentally or planted intentionally. One respondent thought that criminals might learn to use DNA to confuse crime scene evidence. On balance, many respondents thought DNA evidence alone was insufficient to prove guilt because, for example, it did not constitute proof of motivation and/or guilt. Additionally, it was alleged that some police officers might falsely plant biological material at a crime scene to secure a conviction.

6. Other issues

A number of respondents held the view that individual freedoms and 'right to anonymity' were being reduced by the current government. For example, there was deep concern that the NDNAD had become its present size without public consultation. Several perceived this as a move towards a 'police state' and links were made, for example, with the increased use of CCTV, mobile telephone tracking and number plate recognition. Typical anxieties were as follows:

"One easily overlooked aspect is that it can ingrain a culture of providing bioinformation casually without real thought to how important giving unique biometric data can be, and what uses it can really be put to."

Anon

"Some people may say that if you have nothing to hide why not confirm [it] – I'd ask those people if they have curtains in their house (if they have nothing to hide they don't need them!)."

Anon

There was a call by one respondent for better information to be provided to the public on the laws which apply to collection, storage and deletion of DNA on the National DNA Database. The organisation JUSTICE regarded the regulations that govern the retention of DNA on the NDNAD as "a serious interference with fundamental rights" and was concerned that the extent of this interference was significantly underappreciated by the wider public. The response from the Royal College of Nursing raised its concern about the issue of which body should have ownership of the bioinformation collected for police purpose when it was no longer needed for legal proceedings. The response noted that similar issues arose in relation to samples and tissues collected in other settings, such as medical research.

An opposing view was that more weight should be given to the rights of the victims of crime and other threats and less to 'privacy' rights of perpetrators or anybody who came into contact with the criminal justice system. Additionally, it was noted that bioinformation could be used to prove the innocence of a person mistakenly suspected of a crime as well as indicate their presence at a crime scene.

List of respondents

Organisations

Anonymous (1)

Association of Chief Police Officers in Scotland (ACPOS)

Action on Rights for Children (ARCH)

The Association of Police Authorities, the Association of Chief Police Officers and the Home Office (Joint response)

Biosciences Federation and Royal Society of Chemistry

British Academy of Forensic Sciences

British Medical Association

Dr Rob Elles on behalf of the British Society for Human Genetics

Council for the Registration of Forensic Practitioners

Clive Gross, Principal Spokesperson, Eastbourne Green Party

Ecsite-UK

Ethics Committee of the Royal College of Pathologists

ETHOX Centre, Department of Public Health and Primary Care, University of Oxford

Lino Paula, European Commission

The Forensic Institute

The Forensic Science Society

GeneWatch UK

Institut Borja de Bioetica

JUSTICE

Dr Paul Debenham, Director, Technology and Development and Mr Ric Treble, Scientific Advisor, Forensic Division, LGC

Liberty

The London Criminal Courts Solicitors' Association

National Council of Women of Great Britain

Nottingham University Hospitals Ethics of Clinical Practice Committee

The Open Rights Group

Alain Williams, Parliament Hill Computers

The Royal Academy of Engineering

The Royal College of Nursing

Royal College of Nursing, Ethics Forum Steering Committee

School of Applied Sciences, Northumbria University

Senselect Ltd.

Students at Institute of Continuing Education, University of Cambridge

The Wales Gene Park and Techniquest

Wellcome Trust

Individuals

Anonymous (30)
Professor Colin Aitken
Philip G Atock
Professor Barry Barnes, Dr Gill Haddow, Dr Mairi Levitt and Dr Rod Taylor
MIH Becket
Aiden Berry
Mr John Bicknell
Jan Bikker
John Birkett
Benedict Birnberg
Phil Booth
SJ Browne
Dr Bernard Burke
Dr JB Chapman
F Charlesworth
Mr TJ Coldrick
Dave Cook
Colin Craig
Elizabeth Craig
Professor AP Dawid
Mr Graham Dossett
Dr Thomas Douglas
Andrew Evans
Mr Frank Everett
Linden Farrer
Mr Andrew Gretton
Diane Grundy
Rev Dr Daniel Haines
Mr Chris Heatley
Mr Piers Herbert
Paul Higgins
Bob Horner
Joseph Hughes PhD
R Hutchens
Anthony Jackson
Ian Jessiman
Paul A Kendall
Alice Kilroy
Mr J Larmour
IR Ley
A Lloyd
Alexis Manning
Allister Mannion
Mike McGregor
Mr Gavin McIntyre
Dr Meera Manraj
Professor Ben Mepham
Andrew Meredith BEng CEng CITP MBCS MIET, The Anvil Organisation Ltd.
David Mery
Mike Mills
Tony Moeller
Dana Moore
Colin Noad
Robert Nock
Kate O'Mahony
Guy Ottaway
Mr Peter Parry
Ben Pheasey-Rattigan
B Pringle
David Proctor
Sally Ramage
Mike Redmayne
Mrs Helen Sabonjian
Ms Oriola Sallavaci
Satish Sekar
Sarah Smith
Mr Martin Staniforth
Dr Keith Sugden
John Trent
Mr Richard Tyndall
Mr Gordon Walkley
S Ward
Jon Westlake
Tim Wilson
Anthony Wright

Appendix 3: Council of Europe Recommendations on forensic genetic testing

Recommendation R (92) 1 *on the use of analysis of deoxyribonucleic acid (DNA) within the framework of the criminal justice system* (1992) lays down the main principles:

- DNA test samples and results obtained for forensic purposes should not be put to other use, but should be revealed to the subject, given their consent. Medical samples and data should not be put to forensic use except as provided in national law, and data used in research must be anonymised;
- Samples may be taken without the subject's consent, if so provided by national law and if this level of intrusion is proportionate to the circumstances;
- All offences are equivalent, in the sense that the use of DNA tests should not be limited to the more serious cases;
- Testing laboratories must be State-accredited and inspected against criteria of knowledge, skill, quality control, integrity, security and confidentiality, with cited data protection standards being met; standardisation of analytical methods should be promoted;
- The storage of samples and data should be regulated by law. They should generally be held only for the duration of the corresponding criminal investigation, but extended storage is allowed when someone is convicted of a serious offence, and in the interests of national security, if the storage periods are prescribed by domestic law;
- The defence side has rights to DNA results equal to those of the prosecution;
- Nation states should ensure that intellectual property issues do not impede access to the use of DNA analysis;
- The sharing of testing services or results between states should be restricted to states which meet relevant standards, including these principles.

Principle 4.8 of the Appendix to Recommendation R (97) 5 on *the protection of medical data* (1997) is of broader application, since it refers to 'genetic data' rather than DNA analysis. It states that forensic uses of such data should be subject to a specific law offering appropriate safeguards; and also that "The data should only be used to establish whether there is a genetic link in the framework of adducing evidence, to prevent a real danger or to suppress a specific criminal offence. In no case should they be used to determine other characteristics which may be linked genetically."

Appendix 4: DNA Profiling: what are the markers that constitute the DNA profile?

A DNA molecule consists of a long chain of chemical subunits called nucleotides or bases (chemically a base is part of a nucleotide, but for present purposes, the terms can be used interchangeably). There are only four sorts of nucleotide in DNA. They differ according to the base they contain. The bases are adenine, guanine, cytosine and thymine, normally abbreviated to A, G, C and T. Any piece of DNA can be described by listing the sequence of the four nucleotides along one chain. For example, part of one molecule might read:

… GCTGGATTGGTGCCACCTAAAACATTGTTATGCTGGAAATGCTAGAATAT …

Every cell of a person contains 6,000,000,000 nucleotides, and the sequence is the same in every cell of that person.[2] Some variations in DNA affect a person's health or appearance. Some common variants determine things like blood group, eye colour and hair colour – characters that commonly vary between people. Some rarer variants are the cause of genetic diseases like cystic fibrosis or muscular dystrophy. Other variants are believed not to cause disease directly, but to influence the risk a person has of developing common diseases such as cancer or diabetes. However, most variants have no effect at all on a person's health or observable characteristics. The variants selected for DNA profiling have been specifically chosen because, along with other criteria, they are believed to contain no information relevant to a person's health or physical characteristics.

Some 30,000 short tandem repeats (STRs) exist in the human genome. Those used for forensic purposes have been chosen partly because they are particularly variable, so that many different alleles exist in the population. This ensures that match probabilities are as small as possible. Additionally they are selected on the basis of reliably giving clear, well-defined peaks on the laboratory DNA analyser. Each STR in the panel should preferably be from a different chromosome from all others – this helps ensure that match probabilities for each individual STR can be multiplied to give an overall match probability. Originally in the UK four STRs were used. A Second Generation Multiplex (SGM) used six markers. The current SGM+ uses the ten STR markers shown in the table below. It is highly desirable to use the same selection of STRs in different countries, so that profiles can be compared across borders. SGM+ is used in most European countries. The US CODIS set uses 13 STRs, eight of which overlap SGM+.

The discriminating power of DNA profiling depends on the ability to multiply together the match probability from each individual STR. This is known as the multiplicative principle. The procedure is only valid if the alleles of different STRs occur quite independently in the population. Population genetic theory shows that this will only be strictly true if all members of the population interbreed completely freely, which is not the case for any real population. This theoretical point is generally agreed; the controversy is over the extent to which it invalidates match probabilities based on the multiplicative principle. Although in the past the validity of the multiplicative principle was heavily disputed by defence lawyers, especially in the USA, there is no longer major controversy in the courts over this issue. Although it does underestimate the true match probability, it does so to only an unimportant degree.

Markers in the original UK typing set and in SGM, SGM+ and CODIS

Extensive details of these markers can be accessed at: www.cstl.nist.gov/biotech/strbase.

STR	Chromosome	UK first panel	SGM	SGM+	CODIS
D2S1338	2			+	
TPOX	2				+
D3S1358	3			+	+
FGA	4		+	+	+
CSF1PO	5				+
D5S818	5				+
F13A1	6	+			
D7S820	7				+
D8S1179	8		+	+	+
THO1	11	+	+	+	+
VWA	12	+	+	+	+
D13S317	13				+
FES/FPS	15	+			
D16S539	16			+	+
D18S51	18		+	+	+
D19S433	19			+	
D21S11	21		+	+	+
Amelogenin	X, Y		+	+	+
Average match probability		1:10,000	1:50 million	1:1,000 million	$1{:}10^{13}$

Appendix 5: French Comité consultatif national d'éthique – Opinion on biometrics, identifying data and human rights

The French National Ethics Committee, the *Comité consultatif national d'éthique* (CCNE), has examined the uses of biometrics in both civil society and the legal system. Its recent opinion on the subject criticises the law in France for being vague in its description of whose genetic samples could be taken and stored for forensic purposes. It also argues that the criteria for taking and retaining samples is too wide, and that when data are collected there needs to be a purpose "clearly and precisely stated, explained and justified". The approach taken is also one of proportionality:

> " 'The proportionality of means' concept is an essential one since integrating personal data beyond what is really necessary for the stated purpose is clearly unethical."

The Committee also calls for meticulous validation of data to avoid errors, and strict access control to maintain confidentiality. It recommends that all genetic identity databases be placed under the authority of an independent judge (or judges), and the "solemn reaffirmation of the legitimacy of confidentiality protecting personal data, in particular information on physical and sexual characteristics or relating to an individual's family".

Appendix 6: Portuguese Conselho Nacional de Ética para as Ciências da Vida – Opinion on the legal system for DNA profile databases

In June 2007, the **Portuguese National Council of Ethics for the Life Sciences** published an opinion on the legal system for DNA profile databases. It is reproduced below.

The reflection of the National Council of Ethics for Life Sciences (CNECV) on the draft bill regarding the creation and maintenance of a DNA profile database is in response to the request for an opinion from the Under Secretary of State for Justice.

The Opinion of the CNECV is issued under its authority as provided by paragraph b) of clause 1 of article 2, together with what is determined by paragraph c) of article 7, both in Law n.° 14/90 of 9th June.

Considering that,

a. the construction and maintenance of a DNA profile database may constitute an important auxiliary aid for purposes of criminal investigation and civil identification;

b. even though they share a common origin, these two purposes raise important ethical issues with potentially different magnitude;

c. the construction and maintenance of DNA databases reinforces the power and efficacy of the State in matters of security, but may affect the vulnerability of the citizens, namely on safeguards of its rights, freedoms and guarantees;

d. the principal ethical issues concern the criteria for the selection and inclusion of persons, and the collection, conservation, use and circulation of the data;

e. given the sensitive nature of the information, the limitations arising from the methods employed and the permanent consequences of possible laboratory errors, the technical aspects themselves turn into ethical issues;

f. the practical experience of other European countries, such as the United Kingdom or France, whose databases were initially established for precise, restricted criminal purposes, has shown that these purposes were rapidly broadened, through successive legal measures, vulgarising the reasons for their creation and causing concern in the respective societies;

g. the myth of infallibility linked to DNA analysis induces a feeling of false security in the results, which may reduce other more reliable processes of criminal investigation to a secondary level;

h. it is possible to determine the identity of victims and of missing persons through the

they can be used to study the major human ethnic groups. A particular base might be 'A' in some people and 'G' in others. There are about ten million SNPs in human **DNA**. They are catalogued in dbSNP, a publicly accessible database. SNPs are not currently used for routine DNA profiling, but may one day be so used.

subject sample: A biological sample taken from an individual who has been arrested in connection with a **recordable offence**, or a volunteer or victim. This biological subject sample will be profiled to obtain a **DNA profile** for loading onto the National DNA Database (NDNAD).

trace bioinformation: Biological material left behind by an individual (for example, at a crime scene) from which information can be determined (such as a **DNA profile**).

'volume' crime: Crimes that make up the majority of offences recorded in official crime statistics, most often property crimes, and those where victims are likely to report the crime to the police (often to facilitate claiming insurance payments). Most commonly, they include domestic burglaries, vehicle thefts and thefts from vehicles, etc.

Y chromosome: The Y chromosome is present only in men and will remain largely unchanged as it passes through the male line of a family. Different **DNA** variants on the Y chromosome can help with research into the evolution and movement of human populations. Y chromosome profiling is a sensitive means to examine the male-specific component in male/female mixtures, often encountered in rape cases.

List of abbreviations

ACPO	Association of Chief Police Officers
APA	Association of Police Authorities
CCTV	closed circuit television
CJ	criminal justice
CJA	Criminal Justice Act 2003
CJPA	Criminal Justice and Police Act 2001
CJPOA	Criminal Justice and Public Order Act (1994)
CPS	Crown Prosecution Service
DNA	deoxyribonucleic acid
ECHR	European Convention on Human Rights
EGF	Ethics and Governance Framework (UK Biobank)
ENFSI	European Network of Forensic Science Institutes
EU	European Union
FBI	(United States) Federal Bureau of Investigation
FSNI	Forensic Science Northern Ireland
FSS	Forensic Science Service
HFEA	Human Fertilisation and Embryology Authority
HGC	Human Genetics Commission
IPCC	Independent Police Complaints Commission
LCN	low copy number
MTA	Material Transfer Agreement
MtDNA	mitochondrial DNA
NAFIS	National Automated Fingerprint Identification System
NCB	UK National Central Bureau for Interpol
NDNAD	National DNA Database
NFB	National Fingerprint Board
NIDNAD	Northern Ireland DNA Database
NIM	National Intelligence Model
NPIA	National Policing Improvement Agency
PACE	Police and Criminal Evidence Act 1984
PCR	polymerase chain reaction
PED	Police Elimination Database
PITO	Police Information Technology Organisation (no longer in existence)
PNC	Police National Computer

PSNI	Police Service of Northern Ireland
RSS	Royal Statistical Society
SGM	Single Generation Multiplex
SGM Plus (+)	Single Generation Multiplex Plus (+)
SIDS	sudden infant death syndrome
SNP	single nucleotide polymorphism
SOCA	Serious Organised Crime Agency
SOCO	Scenes of Crimes Officers
SOP	standard operating procedure
STRs	short tandem repeats
UK	United Kingdom
UKAS	UK Accreditation Service
USA	United States of America

Index